Books by Donna Bocks

Lavender Blues
Came to Say Good-bye
Heartbeat of Home
Purple Prairie Schooner
Texas Tango
Twin Trees

Home is such
a special place

Donna

Heartbeat of Home

Donna Bocks

Heartbeat of Home

By Donna Bocks

Published by Open Window Creations

Copyright © 2010 by Donna Bocks

All rights reserved. Except for use in any review, the reproduction or utilization of this work in whole or in part in any form by any electronic, mechanical, or other means, now known or hereafter invented, including xerography, photocopying, recording, or in any information storage, or retrieval system, is forbidden without written permission of the author:

Donna Bocks, P. O Box 8231, Holland, Michigan 49422-8231.
DonnaBocks@birthAbook.com

ISBN: Heartbeat of Home: 978-0-9802090-7-5
Project Development: *Open Window Creations*
Cover and Book Design: *Greystroke Creative*
Printed in the United States of America

Copies of this book may be ordered from:
www.lulu.com
DonnaBocks@birthAbook.com

Acknowledgments

How does a 78 year-old get the desire and courage to finally bring her six typewriter-written novels out of the basement, and into the hands of a reader? By reaching out for lots of support!

In the beginning, I was a writer of stories, and received encouragement, feedback, and knowledge from Donna Winters, Dennis Hensley, the Writers Digest School, the Midwest Writers Workshop, and the Herrick District Library Writers Group. Thank you!

In June 2009, I attended a workshop facilitated by Patricia Lynn Reilly, Publishing Coach and so much more. She challenged me to bring my six novels out of the basement and into the hands of a team that produced the book you're holding in your hands! Many thanks to her team of editors, designers, and assistants.

Throughout the years, I've been mother, grandmother, and friend, and my family and friends have supported me, unconditionally. A special thanks to my children and their spouses who joined Patricia's team to illustrate, digitize, and read the typewritten manuscripts on their way into your hands.

Each word in the novel you're reading, expresses my thanks…

For Auntie and the man who loved her…

Part One

Chapter 1

Between fits of laughter, Annie Tucker and a neighbor boy were trying to lug a large box down the front porch steps.

"Easy now," cautioned Annie, as she tried to keep her end from tipping over. "Don't drop this crazy thing after all the struggling we've been through."

"Drop it? I'd rather kick it and stomp on it." He puffed and panted as he juggled his side of the bulky carton. "What've you got in here, anyway?"

"Odds and ends," said Annie. "Mostly 'odds.'"

"No kidding," said the boy, as he guided the box to the trunk of Annie's car. Together they squeezed it in.

"At last!" they both cried in relieved triumph, and with that they fell on the front lawn to rest. Lass, Annie's Shetland sheep dog, assuming it was play time, came bounding toward them, licking their faces. They pushed her away, then struggled back to their feet.

"Where are you off to, anyway?" asked the boy.

"A cottage on Lake Michigan, not far from Tuckerville. It belongs to the family. I have to pack all this junk because we're planning to spend the summer."

"Stay as long as you wish," said the boy, as he accepted some money from Annie. "I'll need to rest up before I help unload this stuff and put it back in your house."

Annie chuckled. "I'll call and warn you in advance. How'll that be?"

She walked back inside the house. Once in her room, she located her journal and jotted down some thoughts.

> 5/27/94 TGIF
>
> Tomorrow is the big day. Aunt Mary, Lass and I will make our annual trek to the lake. Because of trips back and forth during the week, we should be settled in no time. "Yeah! Move 'em out. Get those wagons rollin'."

She tossed the journal up next to her purse. The move was a heck of a job, but it was always worth it because of the low-key atmosphere at the lake. By Saturday noon they should be in the recuperation stage.

• • •

When they arrived at the lake Annie and Aunt Mary sat in the car a few minutes, allowing the stress of moving to work its way out of their bodies. They could feel the release. Then Lass, moving in the back seat, put her right paw on Annie's shoulder and barked. The women laughed. Annie said, "Guess it's time to open the doors and take a deep breath. We made it."

The cottage, north of Holland State Park, added only ten minutes to Annie's driving time to work at her shop in town.

Sunday morning, after a light breakfast, Annie decided to go for a walk along the lake. Aunt Mary had said she was still bushed. Annie spied the sisters, Rosa and Belle, coming down their drive. She had known them since she was a toddler. "Good morning, neighbors. Out for a walk?"

"Hello, Annie, yes we try to walk every day."

"I was heading down Maude's View and up to the footpath along the lake. I used to know some of the people around here when I was a youngster. Lately, it's been the smile-and-wave routine. I know some of the old-timers, but the rest are strangers. I'm ashamed to say we've kept mostly to ourselves in recent years. I think it's time to remedy that."

Annie smiled, then added, "Are you going that way? If so, I'll tag along and you can bring me up to date. You ladies and the Browns are my only close acquaintances."

"Of course we're going your way," said Belle. She stepped out at a lively gait and set the pace for the threesome.

"How about my side of the road today and yours next time?" suggested Annie.

Rosa began, "This place next to the Browns has been for sale for quite a spell. The people still live there, but no one sees much of them these days.

"The tiny place that sets too close to the edge is a rental. Sometimes there are so many cars in the yard you'd think they must all be standing in there like toy soldiers.

"Between renters, and people moving, it seems like we're always seeing unfamiliar faces. You think someone is a stranger and then you discover she lives next door. It seems to be the way of things these days. It's sad."

Annie spoke again. "I have known of some of these people, but never knew them well."

Suddenly, Belle started in with a vengeance. "This is where Maudie lives. She was born here. It's the oldest house, and sets on the highest hill, and that's why this road is called Maude's View."

"We know that, Belle." Rosa shook her head in disgust.

Belle paid no attention, but continued on. "She's short and has red frizzy hair. Someone comes in a couple of days a week to help her in her difficulty, whatever that is. She wears too much jewelry. She's a nosy gossip and has worn out several pair of binoculars."

Annie laughed out loud, and Belle glared at her. "I was laughing at your use of the word gossip. Sorry."

Rosa then spoke in an undertone. "Maude has had trouble walking since birth. She refuses to speak of the problem. Many days she's confined to a wheelchair. Once in a while she can maneuver a walker."

Belle started in again. "Believe me; watching her with that walker makes you sick to your stomach."

They walked up the beach right-of-way and turned onto the lake footpath. There was a hand-carved sign at the turn. Annie could have sworn Belle kicked a little sand in that direction. She and Rosa exchanged glances. Rosa's eyes were pleading for understanding.

"One of my reasons for missing the changes was the years I was off to school. Then, after starting the business, the lake time was scarce and used for relaxing only."

The house that had interested Annie was the castle. The entrance was at the turnoff to Maude's View. The piece of property went from Lake Road through to the water. The section toward the lake was like a park. There was a hedgerow along the beach path and lilac bushes dividing the lake pathway and the yard. There was no mention of the castle or the grounds. They walked on as if it wasn't there.

Annie could sense that Belle had relaxed some. When Belle spoke, it was with a more pleasing demeanor. "The lake is still and peaceful at this early hour. It's like a mirror to the world." Just then a fish jumped. "The mirror has been broken." They all laughed.

Working their way through the woods and out to the Lake Road, they passed the mailboxes and the stone fence that marked the castle land. Eventually that brought them up to the sisters' back yard. They said their good-byes and promised to meet for another walk.

When Annie reached home she sat in her bedroom and jotted some notes in her journal.

> *Rosa—Short, gray hair, sweet personality, little on the plump side.*
>
> *Belle—about 5 ft. 3, colors her hair, slender, was no doubt a nice-looking woman. Her hatefulness is beginning to show in the mean pinched set of her mouth. ??*

The next morning Rosa met Annie at the end of the drive. "Belle is under the weather today. That's not unusual after one of her bad days. She didn't use to act the way she did yesterday. It started a couple of years ago. She became bitter, hateful, and nasty. I've tried to get her to see a doctor but she refuses.

"Most of the time she's okay. She won't talk to me about it. I've talked to my own doctor, because it upsets me. He suggested that possibly she could be having trouble with depression, but he could do nothing without seeing her.

"He wondered if she would talk to a counselor, or her minister. When I mention things like that she gets upset because she doesn't want me to be worried."

There was a woodpecker making lots of noise in one of the trees. Both of the women looked up to see if they could spot him.

With a big sigh, Rosa continued. "When Belle was a young girl she dated a lot. To be honest she was quite the 'belle of the ball.' I envied her. She never married. I'm widowed. I have a daughter and son-in-law and a lovely granddaughter. I think that little girl is the only living person Belle truly loves.

"I apologize, I've gone and ruined our walk in the fresh air."

"No, I just wish I could help."

The silence of the early hour was like a healing balm.

"I almost forgot, you wanted to know about the folks on the other side of the road. The two-story house next to us has a great view of the lake. Its driveway comes off of the Lake Road. Be sure to notice the window boxes over the garage. I think the tenants hire a nursery to fill them.

"The three-bedroom ranch is for sale. Those people have lived there quite a while. Both the large A-frame and the small one are rentals. No one stays long.

"The log house on the corner has a big garden. The folks there seem nice, but I don't know much about them. I just realized that I've told you about the homes but not the people. Changing times, I guess. Even though we stay year-round we make little effort to get acquainted."

Rosa stopped short. "Annie, I think you should drop by to see Maude. She tries hard to be independent. You would like her. She's fun and has quite a vibrant personality. She pushes a little too far sometimes, but I don't want you to miss her because of what Belle said."

"I have to work at the shop tomorrow. Thought I'd stop by the day after. What about the castle?"

Rosa smiled. "That's where John lives. That will take more than one visit. I won't say a word about the castle itself, except that it has an honest-to-goodness moat. What do you think of that? The castle is John's pride and joy. I'll let him share that with you. The lake path runs along the front of his property and delights him. He planted the bushes there so people wouldn't feel they were trespassing. He's a retired veterinarian. A wonderful gentleman with a heart of gold."

"My, that was quite a description. Do I detect some interest there? I didn't hear you mention a wife."

Her face colored, but she denied any interest.

Suggesting they walk in the woods this time, Annie moved across Lake Road and stepped into the scrub pines. "Watch out for poison ivy. I remember being miserable all one summer. That was the year I received my first camera."

"Are the poison ivy and the camera connected?"

"I discovered two baby raccoons climbing in a spindly tree," answered Annie. "The pictures were great but I paid dearly for them. As a rule, cubs remain with the mother one year. They were constantly trilling to one another. I remember wishing I could understand their story.

"Later in the day I returned to the spot. It had rained and they looked like drowned rats. As a youngster I'd wanted to help them, but I decided to let nature devise its own plan for survival."

The women continued to walk side by side.

"If I remember right, there are remnants of a tree house and some forts back in here. This is a beautiful spot."

"You seem to remember a lot about this place," said Rosa.

"Aren't these mushrooms colorful?" said Annie, pointing. "They're big this year. The deer eat some of them. It has been said that the red squirrels take the poisonous ones and put them up in the trees. The rains wash the poison out and after they've dried they're safe for them to eat. Do you think that's just an old wives' tale?"

With big smiles they turned back, picking wildflowers on the way home.

Annie made up her mind: she was going to see Maude. Why not? If Maude was the nosiest old woman in the area, then Annie would get a quick low-down on everyone and everything. Good time management.

Tuesday allowed no time for a visit. Annie had to do the bookkeeping and set up some special orders at the bake shop she owned with a partner. Wednesday, however, Annie took a walk and guided her steps to Maude's.

A voice boomed from inside. "Come on in, Annie, I've been expecting you."

"Do you have spies reporting to you, or what?" Annie adored her from the onset. "Should I call you Maude or Maudie?"

"You've been talking to Chit and Chat, I see. You can call me Shorty for all I care. That's what Clara Belle calls me, and I know it. She's a mean one. Keep an eye on her. Rotten attitude. I'm fixing tea. Help yourself to that big bowl of M&Ms. They have some new colors, you know."

Annie remained in the library as Maude prepared tea in the kitchen. The books were numerous, and Annie found herself scanning the titles.

"You're being awfully quiet in there. You snooping around my house? Do you take cream or sugar for your tea?"

Annie laughed. "Yes, in real life I'm a private investigator. And, no, I take my tea straight. I was looking at your bookshelves. Hey, I see you have a first edition of a Tarzan book. That's marvelous!"

Maude asked for help with the tray of tea and cookies and they settled themselves at the dining room table.

"Maude, this tea is not only delicious, it's a beautiful color. A cadmium orange."

"You probably recognize the cookies. They come from your shop. It's difficult for me to make things like that. I keep some on hand for special occasions."

"Is this a special occasion?"

"Any company is a special event. It perks me up. Tarzan books are a fun read. The one you spotted belonged to my father."

"Listen, I'm a collector, I have twenty of Borroughs's books. I roam through secondhand book shops and antique stores. There're lots of them hiding on old musty shelves. But I have to curb my appetite. If I were to pick them up in one swoop, then what would I do for fun?"

"Flirt with boys," suggested Maude. "Go out on dates. Get married perhaps."

Annie ignored Maude's teasing. "Burroughs wrote a lot of novels. Some were about Mars and two were about Indians."

"Indians?" said Maude, surprised.

"Yep, Indians. Burroughs served in Apache territory with the 7th U.S. Cavalry during the Indian Wars and he later wrote two novels about it, told from the Indians' point of view."

"Well now, you should drop by more often. I could learn a few things."

Annie smiled at that. "May I borrow some of these books from you? I'll bring you some of mine the next time I drop by."

"Good idea," declared Maude. "I love to read but I can't get out to the library or bookstore the way I used to. Help yourself to whatever you see that appeals to you. And don't come back empty-handed."

"You've got a deal," Annie promised. "Now, however, I've got to help you put away these dishes and then I've got to get on my way."

Annie picked up the dishes, then headed for home. She could hardly wait to tell Aunt Mary. She'd like Maude, too. The last comment as she went out the door was meant to sound like it was in jest, but Annie would never forget the words. "Some day if you're bored, come pick me up and we'll search for a wild adventure together." Annie looked up at the clouds. She closed her eyes for a moment and thought, Please let me help. I've got strong legs.

# Chapter 2

Annie didn't take her walk the next morning but instead went right to the stone wall. She had a feeling John was an early riser.

She was about to put her foot on the chain-held drawbridge when a voice said, "Wait for me."

Annie was startled when, almost beside her and stepping out of the moat was the person who had to be John. He had a brown brush cut that was soft and wouldn't stand up properly. His eyes were a burnt brown. A kind face beamed at her. Well-worn work clothes were wrapped around a boxy build.

"There is no water under your drawbridge, Sir John. Instead, I see a multitude of wildflowers of every color."

He clasped her hand. "Join me at the round table, Lady Annie, and I shall tell you the tale of the stone castle." He guided her across the bridge and through the heavy wooden door directly below the turret. "I had heard that you and your Aunt Mary would be joining our little group soon, welcome."

After pouring coffee for her, John brought out large scrapbooks.

"It's all here," said John. "I did research and typed up the information and pasted it on the pages with the accompanying photos."

"When was this place built?" asked Annie, now caught up in the story.

"The first owner built it in 1934," said John, tapping a picture of a whiskered man in the first scrapbook. "He copied its blueprints from the medieval castles of the feudal barons of Europe, only he added such modern conveniences as an indoor bathroom, a telephone, and electricity."

"Ah-ha," said Annie. "A little modernization of history, eh?"

"Exactly," John concurred. "The original structure was one level with a kitchen, bathroom, bedroom, and small living area. It was stone outside and knotty pine inside."

"And the owner lived here?"

"No, not really," said John. "He allowed a family to stay here: a man, his wife, son and daughter. They received free rent in exchange for taking care of the castle and grounds. The tenant was an employee of the Michigan Conservation Department, so he did an excellent job of caring for the place."

"What happened?" asked Annie. "These other photos show the place in shambles."

"Those were taken in 1962, long after the original owner died and the caretakers moved out," explained John. "It sat empty for many years. Animals got inside, rain leaked through the roof, and the grounds became overgrown."

Annie closed the scrapbook. "How'd you find it?"

"Just by chance," admitted John. "I was called out to a farm to help deliver twin calves. I passed by this place and, at once, saw that restoring it would be my retirement project. I bought it for a song, but spent a fortune getting it back in shape. It was worth it. I love my castle."

"Just how bad a condition was it in when you got it?" asked Annie.

John threw up his hands in a sign of despair.

"The whole place was a disaster," explained John. "The windows were boarded up, the door was hanging open. The roof beams had collapsed and were leaning toward the ground. The flooring had disappeared and weeds provided green carpeting. Fortunately, the fireplace was still standing."

John got up and paced as he talked.

"When I looked at those cramped living quarters, I couldn't imagine a family of four residing there. Wires were scattered about. Nasty sayings were scrawled on anything that was solid. They were kind enough to leave the bent-up rusty paint can by the kitchen sink. A mirror still hung above the sink, but you couldn't see your reflection anymore.

"The sink sprouted vines that were creeping up through the drain. One leftover bird's nest added a decorative touch."

Annie shook her head in speechless amazement.

John continued with his story. "It took some doing, but, as I say, I finally was able to arrange to buy the place. First, I dismantled everything, saving anything useful. Then I cleared the land here, keeping as many trees as possible.

"I put a lot of thought into the designing and reconstruction of the building. I wanted to retain the look of a castle, yet have larger, more comfortable rooms. It's lighter inside now because rather than use paneling I painted the walls white."

"Oh yes," agreed Annie, "it's very bright and cheery in here."

"The fireplace was scaled down, and I added an additional bedroom, and a half-bath," said John. "The combination kitchen and sitting area fit the '90s. A microwave oven . . . and an abundance of bookcases, plus substantial closet and storage space. I have it all."

"It's fabulous. You have your spiel down pat. Do you run the tour often?"

John laughed. "Anytime people will listen. I'm meeting friends for lunch, so I need to shower and change. The tour is not complete until you've shared in the ongoing projects between the house and the road. I'd like you to return at your earliest convenience, and the second visit is free."

Annie smiled.

"I'll tell you what, why don't you come up tomorrow morning and have breakfast with Aunt Mary and me. Maybe I can talk her into joining us for the balance of your tour.

 CHAPTER 3

Aunt Mary consented to accompany Annie the following day. She and Annie were eager to discover the secrets of the castle.

John escorted them through the gate. Now he stood back and drew his pleasure from their discoveries. The shed with his equipment was impressive. There was a manmade duck pond, and different-sized fenced-in areas. The coop section and the cages were in excellent shape.

Each area was empty at the moment. But there was enough evidence for anyone to see the care that went on here. If that wasn't enough, one only needed to look at the satisfaction on John's face. Annie saw that as she turned and smiled.

There had been one sad note. John mentioned trouble that had occurred a week ago. Some boys had climbed the fence and destroyed one of the pens. An injured rabbit was gone. A few more days and his foot would have healed completely. John turned partially away from them as he expressed his thoughts. He was hoping it had been set free instead of some of the cruel things he could imagine.

"Luckily I have few trespassers. Basically I treat small animals. If you can catch injuries soon enough the animals can often survive. People in the area know I'm here and sometimes I'm busy helping out. If it's serious I send them to the clinic.

"I hear you have a dog that goes by the name of Lass. I'd love to meet her. Can't have too many friends, you know."

"I can control the land around my castle," said John. "I can trim the trees, plow the gardens, and mow the grass. But I can't control people, if they invade my property and do damage, I'm not as much angered as I am disappointed."

"Well, we're your neighbors," said Aunt Mary. "And you'll never be disappointed in us."

John nodded his head in agreement. "And I'll always be here for the two of you," he promised.

That night Annie turned to a journal page and wrote John's name in the corner. She scribbled:

> *When the name Rosa was mentioned, John's face seemed to display more color than usual. Imagine that.*

Annie and Aunt Mary were beginning to settle in to the cottage. It was okay in town, but the cottage and its colorful neighbors were like an imaginary village. All of the real fun was with John, Maude, Rosa, Belle, and Aunt Mary, she wrote in her journal.

The next morning Annie woke early. The American flag in the front yard was snapping in the wind. Annie dressed hurriedly and left the cottage, hoping to walk in solitude. She headed into the woods. After wandering for awhile she turned back toward home.

Annie thought she heard something. It was hard to tell above the wind. She stood still and listened. There it was, an odd noise, sort of a restrained bawl. Should she hightail it out of there? It was repeated, sounding like a distress call. Annie, very cautiously, tried to locate the source of the noise.

Suddenly, she reached an injured doe and almost stumbled and fell on top of her. She must have gone silent when Annie got close. Her front legs were tied with a piece of strong rope. Someone had been torturing her.

There were burn spots in her fur, as if someone had branded her. A small tree limb had been stuck in her neck and left protruding. It looked like one of her front legs was broken.

Annie backed away and ran toward the road. The rain had started and it was whipping across the pavement. Her chest began to hurt from running so far. She stopped at the stone opening and called for John. He came from out by the pens to see what the commotion was.

She explained what she had seen, as soon as she could catch her breath. John got his bag and a shovel and they climbed into his truck, and went racing down the road.

He pulled the truck on the side of the road where Annie had come from. Minutes later she found the doe again. "John, can we do something?"

"Don't touch anything. Let me prowl around and see if I can get an idea of how this happened. Don't untie the doe. If you see the fawn, you freeze."

"A little one?"

"It will be hidden just a few yards away. I'll be right back."

John returned in a short while looking angry and disgusted. "This is the way I figure it. A car came by on the old road from town. The doe probably ran in front of it and jumped the fence. She broke her leg and fell. Then she stood and tried to get into the woods to hide. The car was pulled over and three sets of footprints followed her. She traveled a short ways and fell again. One of them must have had the piece of old rope in his pocket. Then they started having fun.

"After they left, the fawn was born. The mother cleaned her baby best she could, but it was hard to reach the afterbirth. A fawn can stand in a few hours. It's probably curled up and bedded in some leaves, maybe under a fern. Nature has provided them with perfect camouflage. The mother and the fawn don't bed down together. When they are newborn no odor can be detected. That's also part of the protective system.

"The doe and fawn exchange soft grunts. Mutual grooming provides a bond. That's probably part of the reason the mother seems sedated. The fawn could still nurse."

Annie smiled. "Can I be a vet now, if I take a written exam?"

"There's so much more to it than that." His seriousness deepened as he continued to explain what he thought happened.

It opened another window into John's personality, his heart and soul. The lives of animals were as important to him as his own life.

He returned to his explanation. "I doubt if the men even realized she was carrying the little one. They would have had a field day with that.

"Here's the little fire-pot where they heated the twigs to burn her. They must have started them up with a lighter, because there aren't any telltale discarded match sticks on the ground.

"After what they had done, and being ready to deliver, the doe probably became submissive. That would have spoiled their fun, so they left."

"I hope I don't know a person who would even think of being this cruel."

"Annie, I want you to walk slowly back to the truck. There's an old blanket in the chest in the truckbed. Bring it here. Go on, now."

When Annie returned, John had the fawn in his arms. "Wrap the blanket around him so he can't escape. He's too young to survive without some assistance. If you can carry him, I'd like you to go sit in the truck and wait."

Annie had noticed that John had brought not only his bag but a shovel to the scene. "I'll talk to you about it when I get there. Hurry on and get out of the rain."

After a while John returned to the truck and put his equipment in back. Both Annie and the fawn were shivering.

"How did you find this baby?"

"As I had guessed, he was only a short distance away. I heard his high-pitched mew. He wanted some social contact. Deer feed heavy before a storm, so that was in both their favor."

Annie hung her head, "The mother?"

"She wouldn't have made it. Don't feel bad. Humans feel pain at a greater degree than animals. We have a complex nervous system and our brain is more developed. Trust me, Annie, we did our best." With that he moved the truck onto the road.

"Go home and change into dry clothes," said John. "They had better be old ones if you want to feed this little fella his first meal in captivity. That first bottle can be a struggle.

"I've got to dry him off and get him settled. After that I have to make some phone calls to see the best way to feed and care for him. Also how long before it's safe to release him back in the wild or if that's possible. This day has disturbed things considerably. If he'd been a bit older, he might have made it on his own."

• • •

Laughter was heard more than once echoing from the area of the castle grounds for the next few days. Annie had not only returned that day but during the next couple of days to feed the fawn.

The following Saturday, when Annie returned from work, John was waiting, "Thought you would want to finish our project. On a farm north of us, about twenty miles, there is a small herd of rather tame deer. One of the does had a fawn that was stillborn. We'll drop this little shaver off and let nature take over. There may be a couple of bad days, but it's the only fair chance he'll have."

Annie went along for the ride and was gratified later that day when the little fawn was "adopted" by a new mother. It made all of John's and Annie's efforts seem worthwhile.

During the trip home Annie questioned John as to whether the people who had been so cruel to the deer would be caught and punished. "Most likely not. We are fortunate in this area because most of the people are kind. There will always be a few bad ones.

"Because of lack of funds our police force has been cut back. They are too busy with serious human crimes to pursue such an incident.

"As you know, even a small town like Tuckerville has some horrible situations to deal with."

Silence prevailed after that. Annie was thinking about the beliefs of this person called John. She was glad to know him. He was the kind of individual that made her feel protected from the cruelties of the world. That night she ended her prayers with a thank you for a special friend called John.

• • •

Aunt Mary spent the warm summer days sitting in her white wicker rocker in the yard. She'd pick one of the bright-colored pillows from the porch and get comfortable. The sun warmed her as she watched the boats and listened to the chirping birds. Her favorite entertainment was watching the hummingbird feeder. She got so she could spot the little birds on certain tiny branches. She was always telling Annie how she liked to watch them preen. Often times, however, Annie seemed too busy to watch and listen.

Paying attention to the butterfly bush was another matter. Annie took pictures of the variety of different butterflies so that she and Aunt Mary could enjoy them in the winter months.

Aunt Mary appeared undisturbed and at peace with herself. Annie would sit with her in the evening and watch the sunset and listen to the lapping of the waves on Lake Michigan.

One of the reasons Aunt Mary spent many of her days in the front yard was to escape the noise of the work going on in the cottage. A short time after their arrival they had talked about making a big change in the routine they'd followed in years past and were putting it into action.

They put the house in town up for sale. Annie started winterizing and redecorating the cottage.

The end of July was fair week in Tuckerville. Aunt Mary, Maude, and Annie muddled through the walkways and wolfed down greasy but great-tasting food. Each had an Italian sausage on a bun with onions, green peppers, and sauce. No one wanted to share an "elephant ear," so three were ordered from the wagon, plus lots of napkins. They postponed the lemonade that the man in the booth shook up with sugar; they'd save it for the way home. It would be too much of a struggle to get to the restrooms once they were seated. Besides they didn't want to miss any of the action in the grandstand. After all, it was the night of the harness races. Listening to the announcer was as exciting as the races themselves.

The ride to the cottage was equally fun. Full of laughter, singing "Old McDonald Had a Farm" and other silly songs, and blowing bubbles through the straws into the lemonade. Fair time is fun time, not a grown-up time.

Three exhausted women watched the fireworks from Maude's back porch. They not only could see the bursts, but they could hear them as well; that went for fireworks and mosquitoes.

• • •

August was gone in a flash. In early September the downtown house was sold. A few last-minute things had to be moved. The men at the cottage packed their tools. The makeover was pleasing to the owners, and the men were proud of what they had done. It was time for Annie and Aunt Mary to begin anew.

The porch swing squeaked as Lass struggled up beside Annie, interrupting her daydream. "Well, Lass, are we officially settled?" A tail thumped against the green cushion. Annie gave her a big hug. She was sure Lass was glad that the commotion had gone out the door for the last time.

Aunt Mary brought bowls of tomato soup, crackers, and milk and set them on the small round table on the cottage's screened-in porch. They pulled two chairs up, and Annie blew on her first steaming spoonful. She dropped the spoon back into the bowl and put her hand to her throat. She was staring out through the screen.

"Fire!" The sparks were shooting to the tops of the trees. Annie almost yanked the hinges off the newly hung door. Racing to the top of the hill, she stumbled. What was burning?

She looked over the edge. The neighbors glanced up and motioned for her to join them at the bonfire. Shaking her head no, she hoped they couldn't see the panic she was feeling. What did she think was on fire: Lake Michigan, or the storage building on the beach?

What was the matter with her? She felt like she was unraveling like an old worn-out sweater.

Annie marched back to the cottage. Explaining the scene to her aunt, she stated, "I'm going to finish my soup and then go to bed. I've had enough excitement. I feel brain dead."

She pushed her shoes off, and minutes later she was sound asleep. Her usual care of that pretty new comforter she had ordered from the J. C. Penney catalog went by the wayside.

Hours later Annie became restless and turned over to look at the clock. It was after 1:00 a.m. She remained still, listening. The cottage was silent. Aunt Mary and Lass were worn out, too.

She was still weary but not sleepy now. Sitting up, she looked around the room. This is home, she thought.

Quietly, she reached for her journal and pen, which were lying on the antique smoking stand. It was the only remembrance Annie had kept of her father.

She felt the softness of the new carpeting on her feet. It was still warm enough for windows to be left open. That luxury would last only a few more nights.

Settling in on the porch, she pulled the canvas chair up by the table and sat down.

Annie realized that she had become highly organized in her adult life, but that it had taken a long time before she had headed in that direction. Tomorrow would be new. But now, she wanted to examine the past.

She hadn't written in her journal since the deer incident. This was a good opportunity to get caught up. She smiled. All things considered, her memories were to be celebrated.

Her thoughts wandered back to what had taken place all those years before the journal.

Annie could barely recall her life before living with Aunt Mary. There had been the nice three-bedroom ranch home on Green Street in Tuckerville. When it got sticky in the summer they avoided the town, enjoying the cottage and its relaxed atmosphere.

Aunt Mary, her mother's older sister, had been widowed and was frequently at the house. In fact, she had been looking after Annie when the policeman had come to the door to inform them of the plane crash that had taken her parents.

Aunt Mary sold her house nearby, and she and Annie were family from then on. For Annie, at the age of four, the adjustment fell into an easy pattern.

Aunt Mary had repeatedly held Annie in the rocking chair, telling her about her family. It was better than a picture book.

She told her how Tuckerville had been settled by someone way back in the family. Her grandfather had established Tucker Trucking. Her father, though a young man, was a great organizer. That's why the trucking business could thrive even now, in his absence.

Aunt Mary was matronly and perfect for the job. Her hair had been white as long as Annie could remember; one braid was always across the top of her head. Aunt Mary always had on a coverall apron. She made them herself, cutting the patterns out of newspaper.

Often there would be company for meals. On Sundays the aroma of chocolate fudge drifted about the house as it cooled in a pie tin. Once in a while Aunt Mary would add peanuts. In the evening she'd peel apples, with the peelings falling into a big red bowl. The apples would be quartered and passed to whoever wanted a bite.

A living angel. Just to be near her was consoling. After Annie had reached 5 feet tall, as measured on the door casing of her room, they decided not to keep track anymore. But during the last trip to the house, she had spotted a note taped by the marks.

> *Plus 4 in. About 120 lbs. Ratty jeans Logo T shirts Also likes umbrella and dressing up*
> *Has a happy disposition (Our Girl)*

The new owners would get a kick out of that. Annie thought of removing it. But she didn't.

Annie recalled her curiosity at a young age about the trucking business that supported her and Aunt Mary. At first the management and employees thought her showing up and asking questions was a novelty. It didn't take long for them to realize she wasn't someone they could pass off with simple explanations.

She soon learned every phase of the business. Annie seemed to follow in the footsteps of her father. She acquired the same knack of productive organization. She learned how to keep workers happy, also when to step in on a personal level. But she never interfered. Her father had appointed a fine man as manager.

As a graduation gift for Annie, the staff and workers, using their own money, threw an unsurpassed wingding. A smile covered Annie's face when she remembered that fun-filled evening.

Following that was confectionery school. Hello, Lottie Anderson from

Beaufort, North Carolina. Crazy, imaginative, fun-loving Lottie. They had spent their senior spring break in Beaufort: their last fling of freedom. And here it was 1994. Lottieannie's Confectionery had been a success since it opened its door two years ago.

Tuckerville's downtown had been reestablished after the influx of malls. Quaint gift shops for the tourists were flourishing. The area was growing, too fast.

As co-owners, Annie and Lottie worked well together. The sign in the window claimed:

**Frivolous-Delicate-Elaborate-Luxurious
We can create it. Especially, if it's CHOCOLATE.**

On the porch table, the journal lay untouched. Maybe she'd catch up someday. The important thing was she felt caught up in her mind.

In between the clean sheets, Annie slept soundly until her alarm rang at 6:00 a.m.

The late September sun presented a promising day. At breakfast Annie folded her arms and posed a question. "What about the note on the door at Green Street?" Aunt Mary smiled, and softly said, "I felt we might be leaving that girl behind." Conversation stopped with that.

They sat back to enjoy a second cup of coffee. Annie looked at that wise and kind person who meant the world to her. She carefully worded another question. "In early summer, when we came to the cottage, I thought we decided we wanted to stay permanently. Was I mistaken?"

"Not at all. We both love it here. It's just that at age twenty-four the girl in you has gone. I love you just as you are, but I miss our girl. She has become a woman without my noticing."

Again the conversation ceased. Annie kissed Aunt Mary on the cheek and said, "Take it easy today."

 CHAPTER 4

Twenty minutes after Annie arrived at the Confectionery she realized that her heart wasn't in work. She needed a "skip day." She grabbed up the phone and called Aunt Mary back at the cottage.

"This is me. We need a day off. It's been a tough summer. Work has really been rolling. You have been cooking and unpacking, in spite of the high temperature. Lass is uncomfortable in the heat. We've been living in the midst of a mess, with the builders working around us. It's over. It's what we said we wanted. Now we need some rest. We must go shopping for some big pins to wear that say, 'We Survived.' Are you still there?"

"Well, Miss Annie Tucker, your news bulletin isn't very newsy. You just left here. How could you be at work? Those Rockport boots of yours are pressing down too hard on the gas pedal."

"It only takes fifteen minutes to get to town. I'm going to come and get you for lunch. Have you ever been to the Tea Room?"

"I haven't, but have heard inviting reports from friends."

"Press your anticipation button and try to keep yourself under control until I get home at noon."

The Omni pulled up by the back door right on time. Aunt Mary climbed in and got settled. They drove back to the Lake Road and Annie turned left.

"I'm going to Holly's Landing to get gas. When I go in to pay I want to check things out.

"We've got to get better acquainted now that we're out here to stay. Want to come in for a few minutes, Aunt Mary?"

"No, I'll just wait here, thanks. Take your time."

Annie stepped inside and looked around the familiar setting. It was the one place that seemed to remain the same no matter how much things changed around it. Truthfully, it was getting a rundown look. Rundown or dilapidated.

The stools at the counter were full. As she looked from face to face, Annie began to grin. No, nothing had changed. It was still like an old general store.

"The coffee still the best in the county, gentleman?" Six coffee mugs were raised in salute.

"I heard you were gonna be around full time now. Where is that pretty aunt of yours?" asked a man wearing a John Deer cap.

"Is this the Annie who ran in here screaming when she was a little tyke because there was a snake sunning itself on the pavement?" asked a second man, just before biting into a doughnut.

"No, she's the skinny twelve-year-old who sat on the end of the dock kicking her feet in the water and scaring the fish away," said the first man, laughing.

"Okay, you guys, you've got me pegged. Aunt Mary is in the car. She's waiting for me. I'll tell her you said hello."

"Do that," the men chorused as Annie left.

The two women rode in relaxed silence. The warm and friendly sun was keeping its promise. Fall was a fine time of the year. And today was for sharing.

"Here we are, Country Garden Tea Room. You're in for a treat." Annie held the door and watched Aunt Mary's face light up. "Come on, I'll give you a tour. I see that Kate is busy with a salesman."

"Well, I never! No," Aunt Mary insisted, "just let me take it all in. Don't say a word."

Annie watched Aunt Mary's eyes glance around the room and could guess what she was thinking. Tea, coffee, gifts, cards, an Agatha Christie corner with a couple of comfortable chairs. Another corner stuffed with bears of every size and shape. Some sitting in old children's rockers. White linen clothes, goblets, china. There were flowers everywhere. It was like stepping into another world. There were baskets scattered throughout, many of them filled with display items.

The sign above the cash register read:

11:00-3:00 7 days a week
Serving Light Luncheons
With a fantastic finale
Specializing in Courtesy

Annie guided Aunt Mary out to the small herb and flower garden in the back. They could enjoy the charming umbrella tables. A lovely girl stopped to pour a cup of friendship. Aunt Mary pointed to an item on the menu. "What is Marigold bread?"

Annie told her, "It's like nut bread, with edible flower petals. Excuse me, I've got to speak to Kate concerning an order."

Annie found Kate in the kitchen area. "How's that Butter Brickie selling?"

"It's going as fast as the hard version. Some people prefer it. Easier on the dental bill. The taste is just as habit forming. It's hard to leave it alone once you've tried a piece, as you well know. Pretty soon folks will start referring to me as fat Kate. I need a new supply. Also some of the other chocolates need to be filled in. Plus, I'm getting low on the Tea and Roses

Cheesecake."

"Our shops are not far from one another. I'm surprised these items aren't in competition," said Annie. "But it seems to work just the opposite. Instead of competing, they seem to complement each other. Good for you, good for me. Can't beat it. I'll tell Lottie. I'm glad you prepare everything else. You keep us busy with these few items."

"I'm going to walk out with you," said Kate. "So I can enjoy Aunt Mary's company for a few minutes." On the way they paused to speak to a table of three men. Annie observed Kate move gracefully, pausing to talk to guests. The wide-brimmed hat accented her long flowered dress with the full-length white cotton apron. She filled the role of Tea Lady.

Aunt Mary's first question when they were seated came as a surprise. "Kate, why did you introduce Annie to that table of men as a good friend? You are a relative."

Annie laughed. "Let me answer that. She does it by request. I feel that a relative is given to you, a friend is earned."

They ordered, Aunt Mary changing her beverage to iced tea. She then beamed and declared, "Kate, no wonder you retired early from teaching to fulfill your dream."

Kate's smile slipped a bit and she looked seriously at Aunt Mary. "Tell you a secret. It's hard to be this charming all the time. Too often my family suffers because of it. But I do enjoy it. Maybe you could come in and relieve me a couple of days a week. I'm not joking. Think about it." She glided away but looked around with a good-bye smile.

After a nice lunch of tossed salad with grilled fish, and later some warm apple pie à la mode, Aunt Mary took a few extra minutes to look around the tea room. Its elegance appealed to her.

She bought a small package of fine imported apricot tea. It was the same as that used for their special iced tea served this day. She had used her lemon wedge and one packet of artificial sweetener: very satisfying. It wouldn't taste the same at home, but every time she fixed it would remind her of this memorable time with Annie.

On the way out she said, "Thank you, sweetheart, that was delightful. I think that takes care of not only today's meals but tomorrow's also."

Annie smiled radiantly. "I'm glad you liked it. Kate's food is always delicious and her eye for decorating is marvelous. This is a great place. Makes you feel like you've been out on the town. Hey, what did you think about her offer for you to be a part-time hostess?"

Aunt Mary shook her head. "Oh, I'll think about it, I suppose, but for now I'm content the way things are."

As they passed the blueberry fields on the way home, it was Aunt Mary's assigned job to watch for deer.

Turning off the Lake Road, they pulled up by the mailboxes. Waving at John, they started up Maude's View. Just two houses down, Annie slammed on the brakes. Indignantly she remarked, "I've never seen that dog before. I don't know why this is a convenient spot for dropping off pets." The yellow Lab watched their car for a couple of minutes then ran into the woods.

As she pulled in the yard and up by the steps to the kitchen, Annie glanced sideways. She realized she had been talking to herself. Aunt Mary was nodding off. Even a possible disaster wasn't going to keep those eyelids open.

The following evening they were invited next door to the Browns' cottage. Mr. Brown opened the door before they had a chance to knock. His wife hurried from the kitchen, wiping her hands on a towel. Annie had known these people since she was very young. To her they were Mr. and Mrs. Brown or the Browns. She had never called them by their first names.

Mrs. Brown said to them, "If we hadn't decided to stay into the fall this year we wouldn't have had a proper visit at all. Here it is October first, and we are packed to leave in the morning. I told Mr. Brown we must have you for supper to catch up before we left."

Now Annie recalled part of the reasoning behind the names. They referred to each other as Mr. and Mrs. Bubbly and well-meaning Mrs. and helpful Mr. Brown. Supper was good. After eating they all moved onto the porch before ending the pleasant evening.

"I'll miss the seagulls, and my pair of doves. It's hard to concentrate," claimed Mrs. Brown. "I've spent half my day out here trying to count the Canadian geese flying over."

Aunt Mary laughed and said, "Speaking of birds, early this morning I noticed the birds were having a skating party on our birdbath. Time to turn it over, I guess."

Mr. Brown stood and nodded. "I'll turn that birdbath for you. Then we need to get to call it a night."

The three women exchanged hugs. The last word was by Mrs. Brown. "One thing I won't miss is the smell that comes down from the lumber company in Muskegon when the air is heavy."

That produced laughter. They waved good-bye and promised to spend more time together the next summer.

It had been a nice fall, and many of the summer folks had delayed their departures. The cold weather renters were beginning to move in along the water. Locals could feel Indian summer hiding behind the trees in the woods, waiting. Still the sun shone. Summer was not quite ready to relinquish its hold. But the cold nights were becoming more frequent.

 CHAPTER 5

At mid-morning on Monday Annie's phone rang. Aunt Mary had gone to a meeting with some ladies. Annie was working on her computer. The phone almost had an emergency sound to it. She snatched it up, "Yes, may I help you?"

"Oh, one of those days is it? Stop what you are doing and move your body to the front yard."

"Maude, I'm busy."

"You told me you were an Edgar Rice Burroughs fan. Move your fanny out of that chair. If you bustle a bit you will catch a glimpse of the Lord of the Jungle rising from the lake."

Annie carried the portable phone, but was thinking, I wonder if she drinks? Maybe it's a joke.

She stood at the edge of the grass, looking at nothing. That instant, out of the water, rose the Lord of the Jungle. Annie stood with her mouth hanging open, phone by her ear. He looked up and waved; Annie curtsied. Lass sat beside her. "What do you say, girl, friend or foe?" The dog's tail swished back and forth.

She hurried back onto the porch. "Maude, he waved, I curtsied like a little girl at her first recital. I was just standing there. He's probably invading the planet and no doubt thinks we all come with a phone built in one ear. Maude, who is that? If I had thought you were telling the truth I'd have slipped on my leopard leotards."

Maude was laughing so hard she could barely respond. "Don't raise your voice to me, girl. I don't know who it is. But I'm going to ask around. Over and out."

All was lost as far as working at the computer at home. Annie left a message on her answering machine telling Maude to call her at work if there were further developments.

Pausing at the mirror on the way out, Annie studied her face. She wore very little makeup, had a turned-up nose, and there was a chip out of a front tooth, a result of sticky candy. Would Tarzan be interested in someone like that? With a foolish grin, she ran to the car.

The day dragged on and on. Aunt Mary didn't make any comment after Annie returned home. So she rang Maude's number. There was nothing to report. He had disappeared as soon as he was spotted. What a disappointment.

Annie and Aunt Mary had put sweaters on and were sitting on the porch munching apples and watching the beginning of the sunset.

"I beg your pardon."

Annie was so startled she nearly choked on a piece of apple. It was him. She jumped up but made no sound.

Aunt Mary came to the rescue. "Come in, young man. Would you care for an apple?"

"No thank you. I didn't mean to frighten you. I'm Michael Hillerman." He shook hands with each of them. Annie sat down. "I guess you didn't hear me when I walked up."

Annie was studying him. He was quiet but had a commanding personality. He had long dark hair, wore brown pants and a flannel-lined jeans jacket. The reason she hadn't heard him approach was the moccasins.

His eyes were mesmerizing and observing. She could swear he was seeing things about her that she didn't allow anyone to see. It was as if he knew more about her than she did herself. Uncanny. She shuddered. Was it from the chill of the evening?

She then realized she hadn't uttered a word. "I apologize. I haven't been very polite. Are you renting in the vicinity?"

"I'm staying in the woods a few days.'

"You're kidding."

His smile seemed to involve his whole face. "No, I have a very close friend who is an Indian. In the past we've camped out many times. I wanted to ask a couple of questions. Is the beach area private or can I swim and jog freely? Also, am I on private property in the woods? I don't want to get into trouble or cause people to complain."

Annie's tongue loosened up. "I'm sure no one will complain. Just don't start any fires."

"Well, I had better head back. See you tomorrow."

"Sure thing," Annie mumbled.

Aunt Mary sat quietly rocking.

A few minutes passed and Annie darted for the phone, dialing Maude's number. "Hello agent M, this is agent A reporting." After she had hung up she told Aunt Mary the full story.

Her aunt's eyes twinkled. "A little excitement in the neighborhood to spark up the place."

The phone rang at daybreak. "He jogs." The phone went dead.

Annie hurried outside. He had been found out. News travels fast. The lines must be humming. It's a wonder he wasn't blinded by the reflections from binoculars, and it wasn't a bit surprising. A beautiful body, muscular, shirtless. Yes indeed, a fine specimen. He waved and she returned a combined wave and salute.

Before the store opened, she and Lottie caught up on the happenings.

"What a body."

"You've seen his body?" asked Lottie.

"He jogs the beach early in the morning."

"Does he now? Ah-ha!"

"His lips look soft and inviting," said Annie.

"He's kissed you?"

"Lottie, pay attention. They look inviting."

As they locked the door at the end of the day Lottie told her, "Tomorrow morning I'll stop by at the cottage early to see if you want me to bring anything down to the office."

"See you bright and early then," called Annie. "You will love his high cheek bones." She laughed heartily as she climbed into her car.

By Thursday Michael Hillerman was a phenomenon, the local Pied Piper. Children and mothers were fascinated. He was quite the naturalist. The men were skeptical. Annie thought the whole thing great sport.

Just as they were going to shut the cottage up for the night, there was a tap at the door. Annie could see his face through the glass. Opening the door she said, "You're calling late this evening."

"I had some things to do and just got back. I was hoping I could catch you. John says they have a canoe for rent at the Landing. I want to check some things out on Pigeon Creek. Would you care to join me for breakfast down there and a cool morning ride?" Michael shivered as he spoke.

Hesitation would have been proper, but Annie couldn't do it. "Come on over in the morning and I'll drive us down." Annie called Lottie to cancel the morning stop-by; she didn't wanting to explain why. She was relieved when the answering machine clicked on.

 CHAPTER 6

The next morning wasn't cool, it was downright cold. It was also quiet and beautiful. Annie had never been on Pigeon Creek at this time of year. It was foggy at the beginning. They could hear some trawlers but couldn't see them. Annie started the conversation. "So, you've met John."

"Actually, I've spent quite a bit of time with him. He's one fine fellow. Had lunch with Maude yesterday. She's really a character. She seemed pleased that I stopped by."

"I doubt if pleased is an adequate word. So, you've been out and about. How is the campsite working out?"

He put his finger to his lips. From then on they listened. The sun broke the haze and they were gliding in the midst of the swans. Annie remained silent and didn't move a muscle. Michael barely touched the paddle to the water and drifted away. The swans had remained. What a fantastic moment. Certainly a rare and touching experience. By noon they were back at the cottage.

As he left he called back, "See you at the bonfire tomorrow evening."

Annie walked past her aunt, laid on her bed and began to cry. Aunt Mary came to the doorway. "What's wrong honey?"

"Not a thing Aunt Mary, not a thing." Soon she was asleep. After a time Annie began to dream. When she started to waken she could not remember details but there was a smile on her face that she could not erase.

The men got the fire started early and people began to gather. Somehow John had transported Maude to the fun. Rosa and her daughter, son-in-law, and granddaughter joined in, and even Belle decided to attend.

They started to compare the difference between the humidity of the past summer and how good the bonfire felt this evening.

"Let's play 'Can You Top This' with our humidity stories," someone called out. The speaker started things off with, "It steamed my glasses all the time."

"It made all the pictures in our house get crooked."

"The fire alarm kept buzzing and scared the dog."

"I felt so logy."

"Is that a grandma kind of word?"

"Coffee filters were limp."

"So was the toilet paper on the roll."

"My drawers were stuck."

"Let's keep the party clean."

"My scales went crazy and everyone in the house weighed 300 pounds."

Rosa's granddaughter came running up out of breath. "Auntie Belle, my eyebrows itch. Does that mean I'm starting to grow up?"

"I think that's a good question," someone stated.

With that, they all started roasting hot dogs. One of the boys came up to offer Annie a marshmallow that looked like a piece of charcoal.

"Oh, no thanks, I like mine just lightly browned."

"Maybe this one will do, my lady." Michael offered it with a big sweeping bow.

"Are you Prince Valiant tonight?"

"I thought you were with your pageboy hair cut, Annie."

Everyone laughed at that. Annie and Michael stepped back from the fire a little.

"I had begun to think you had changed your mind, Michael."

"I couldn't find my baseball cap and it's getting colder."

Aunt Mary stepped closer to them and said loud enough for several people to overhear, "Michael, you will freeze your cheeks if you stay in the woods tonight. Why don't you come and sleep in our downstairs room. There's a bathroom down there, too."

Soon the fire burned down, and most of the crowd headed homeward.

As they neared the cottage, Michael put his hand on Aunt Mary's shoulder. "You know, I like hot chocolate before turning in." So, hot chocolate it was. The combination of fresh air and the bonfire had made them all sleepy.

Aunt Mary and Annie were surprised in the morning when they heard no stirring from below.

Annie went slowly down the stairs with an empty feeling inside. The bed was made up and on the pillow lay a sprig of Sweet Annie, from the back yard. Annie sunk into a chair. A few minutes later she realized Aunt Mary was standing by her side. At breakfast Annie looked at her aunt and sadly asked, "Do women ever quit having schoolgirl dreams?"

"Not if they're healthy."

Maude phoned later in the day. Annie heard Aunt Mary tell her that Tarzan had returned to the jungle. Annie cherished the memory of the swans on Pigeon Creek. However, the visit of the stranger was never mentioned again.

• • •

The shop was bustling. Holiday orders and supplies were flowing. Annie and Lottie were lining up some part-time help to cover the rush. Working hours were increasing. Annie's heart was beating a little faster. The season was upon them.

Annie was tired but exhilarated as she drove home. Rosa was at the mailboxes, and Annie stopped to pick her up.

"I have your mail here too Annie."

"Aunt Mary didn't come down to get it?"

Rosa didn't respond until Annie pulled up to let her out. She then reached over and placed her hand on Annie's. "Don't pull back on the road yet. Aunt Mary hasn't been picking up your mail." She sat quiet for a minute. "There is no good way to say this," she warned. "Your aunt is dying of cancer."

Annie had the sensation that a frenzied animal was disemboweling her. Her flesh seemed unoccupied, like a dress flung in the laundry basket. Leaning forward, she folded her forearms across the top of the steering wheel and laid her head against them.

Rosa put her arm across Annie's shoulder. Nothing needed to be said.

"How long has she known?"

"I've taken her for several tests and today the doctor gave her the prognosis. It's spreading like wildfire. She may only have six weeks."

"Rosa, you've got to help me."

"The doctor said he would contact hospice. You are going to need them. Belle and I are right across. Don't worry, we'll all help."

Annie opened the car door; put the mail in one hand and her briefcase in the other. She didn't know if she had enough strength to walk the few feet to the cottage.

Her aunt had supper simmering and she was setting the table. Annie handed her the mail, saying that Rosa had picked it up.

"By the look on your face I'd say she also spilled the beans."

They fell into each other's arms, searching for comfort. "We've been a team for a long time, Aunt Mary. To whom will I give the little statue, the award? The one that is inscribed: 'Thank you for your patient understanding and for being a great listener.'" With that they pulled apart and laughed.

Through her tears Annie claimed, "I'm not worried about you. I'm confident that you will make it through this, displaying your wonderful self. It's myself that makes me fearful."

The initial shock had passed, for now. While trying to eat a little something, they talked about it as if they were making out a grocery list.

"Hospice is coming to see us tomorrow afternoon. I want to continue doing everything I can until I run out of steam. There's so little time. My desire is to enjoy every minute I can."

The next day, after the hospice representatives left, there were immediate and radical changes. Still, attempts were made to keep things as close to normal as possible. Annie insisted on cheerful visitors only. It was amazing to see the unlimited pleasantries the residents of Maude's View devised.

Those first weeks were full of remembering for the two women. One night Aunt Mary became very serious. "Oftentimes I have referred to you as 'our girl.' At first, I thought it was because I shared you with your parents. As the years passed I almost felt as if you had been conceived in my own marriage. Will you forgive me?"

"Forgive you? For loving me? Never. I must relinquish my spot now, for one of the children from down the way has come to read you a bedtime story."

A month later they were forced into a more subdued existence.

Annie watched the hospice ladies administer their gentle care. She observed the tenderness shown for the mind of a body that was visibly trying to shut itself down, like a complicated machine running out of fuel. The emotional support they provided for Annie was a godsend. She thought they must each be loved in order to give of love so completely.

They even made an effort to pet Lass each time they came by. They anticipated needs and fulfilled them in a way that seemed like an everyday occurrence. Annie often watched as they went to depart to see if she could catch a glimpse of their "angel wings." Their caring could not be surpassed. Their dignity gave dignity to the patient.

Lass kept out of the way, as if she knew the seriousness of the situation. Every night before she went to her basket she tottered in to say good night to Aunt Mary.

One evening Annie went to Aunt Mary's room to make sure she was covered and warm for the night. She bent down to kiss her soft cheek. All of a sudden, Aunt Mary took her hand and with surprising strength, pulled her close, wrapping her arms around her shoulders. Her voice was raspy when she spoke. "I don't believe I will be here in the morning and I wanted you to know that I love you."

Annie gulped and quietly left the room. It was a farewell to store in her heart. Wrapping a blanket around herself, she sat in the overstuffed chair staring into space until she fell to sleep.

The December sun shone in the window. The dog's basket was empty. Annie tiptoed to the door. Lass was snuggled up by Aunt Mary, her head lying gently on her cold hand. What better company to see Aunt Mary off on such a journey.

The funeral was simple, as Aunt Mary would have wanted it. There were faces Annie had never seen. Stories she had never heard. Accounts of kind deeds and endless hours of help. Annie wondered, Had she been too busy with her own life to notice this woman's dedication, not only to her, but to countless others?

There was still a lot to learn, and now Annie must learn it alone.

Work was piling up in town. Enough burdens had been placed on Lottie. Digging in deep with a heavy work schedule would help square things and keep Annie's mind busy. Being with people and a different atmosphere would help absorb the pain of loss.

It was mid-December, snowing and blowing, winter having set in for sure.

Annie was about to feed Lass her breakfast when she realized the dog was missing from her basket again. Hurriedly she checked each room. Finding her curled up in the middle of Aunt Mary's bed, Annie was relieved. She appeared natural, but before Annie took one step toward her she knew. She threw on her old jacket and boots and trudged to John's, leaning into the wind. Lake Michigan sounded like a locomotive.

Annie pounded on the heavy door. When John opened it, Annie just stood there. She raised her head, and he gently pulled her inside. "It's Lass."

"I'll hurry and get my bag."

"No need to hurry. She's gone. Died of old age." With that said, Annie slid to the floor. John picked her up and put her on the sofa.

Annie could hear someone mumbling and sobbing. It sounded far away. If only the train wouldn't make so much noise. Whoever it was kept repeating something about the ground being frozen. She thought she saw John hurry across the room. He was talking. He sounded upset. Then she couldn't hear or see anything.

"Can I talk to Rosa?" asked John into the phone.

"No! Talk to me."

"Belle, listen to me. It's Annie. Apparently, her dog has died. Annie walked down here. She seems out of her head. Everything has piled up on her. We need some help."

When Annie's eyelids fluttered open, the anxious faces of John, Rosa, and Belle gradually came into focus.

"My Lass is gone, too. Doesn't God want me to have anybody?" It was spoken with the voice of a small and frightened child.

Belle reached for Annie's jacket and took charge of the situation. "John will take care of good old Lass. You are to come home with Rosa and me for a couple of days. John will drive us up to the house."

And so it was. Annie was put to bed for two days. She was filled with homemade soup. Love was delivered by the carload.

The third day she escaped to the store. Lottie was obviously delighted to see her. Annie spent any free moment that day putting together a box of sweets to deliver to two special ladies. She stopped on the way to give John a big bear hug.

Her hands were wrapped around a steaming mug of coffee when she caught her first glimpse of the deer in the yard. "Aunt Mary, come quick." How often would this happen? No Lass to share it with either. Annie located her journal. Jotting down only the facts of the loss of her two closest friends was all she could force herself to do.

 CHAPTER 7

The phone jangled Annie's nerves, but she picked it up with relief. "It's me dear, calling from busy old Chicago. Mr. Brown and I want you to spend Christmas with us. You can pop up Saturday. We'll have a quiet Christmas day. The day after, we are having a get-together for a few close friends."

"By golly, it sounds good. I may not be the best company, but I sure need a change of scenery," Annie answered enthusiastically.

That weekend Annie was helping with minor preparations for the Browns' party. The lid was popped off of a peanut can and Annie snitched a peanut or two. In doing so one rolled across the kitchen floor.

Annie was trying to retrieve it from under the table. Mrs. Brown said, "Our first guest has arrived. This is Mike." She hurried toward the sitting room as the doorbell rang.

Annie noticed the shine on the casual dress shoes. The pants were corduroy. On his wrist was one of those fancy watches that tells you what color underwear is selling in Tokyo. By this time Annie was crawling out from under the table. Her eyes were taking in the good-looking sweater and the open-collared shirt. Annie was about ready to break into a welcome smile, when her eyes reached the well-trimmed hair and clean shaven face. All that remained were the eyes. When their eyes met the peanut can fell to the floor and bounced across the room.

"Hello Annie."

Mrs. Brown walked into the room to the sight of peanuts rolling all over the kitchen.

"Who are you?" Annie was holding onto the edge of the counter to steady herself.

"Do you two know each other?"

"Mrs. Brown, do you have a spot where Annie and I could have some privacy from the rest of your guests? We have some talking to do."

"Yes, there's a tiny room we use as a library. It's out of the way and no one will bother you. Come with me." Michael took hold of Annie's arm.

Mrs. Brown stood in the hallway looking puzzled. Michael very slowly closed the library door.

Annie sat down heavily on the comfortable loveseat. Michael continued standing. She couldn't even look at him. To dispense with the tension in the air she blurted out, "This is a classy high-rise. It presents a nice view of the city lights." She jerked her head up and looked directly at him. "Say something, Michael, anything."

"I don't know where to start."

"Start by telling me who you are and what you were doing in our woods."

"I'll start off by saying that I lied to no one. Nor did I misrepresent myself. John was the only one who knew my purpose in being there."

"He never said a word."

"I didn't think he would. My roommate in college was the Indian friend I spoke of. He taught me survival, and the wonderful mysteries of nature."

Annie spoke up, "You cut quite a figure jogging on the beach. Everyone was fascinated and frightened at the same time. The women were afraid you were going to lure their children away. The men thought you were going to seduce their wives. You were observed at all times. Some thought you were casing the area. You really slept in the woods and not in a motel?"

Mike laughed. "I found a great spot in your woods. At night I would gaze up at the stars and think. By the way I did have an offer from a woman renting a cottage over the winter, but it was an offer I refused."

Annie snorted and clapped her hands, but then turned serious. "So, what was your purpose in being there? Should I call you Mike or Michael?"

"I'll leave that up to you. I was doing some research for a thesis for my psychology class. The professor said the assignment was open-ended; we could do anything we chose to do. I decided to try to come up with something out of the ordinary."

By this time Annie was transfixed and Michael had her complete attention.

"I decided to write about human behavior, reactions to unexpected happenings. How people in the '90s would accept a stranger in their midst. It was a comparison to the '30s when hobos stopped at houses looking for odd jobs. Are you listening?"

"I'm sorry, I was thinking of how the swans accepted us, as long as we didn't disturb their way of life."

"I didn't feel I should stay any longer. The professor was very impressed with my paper."

"Did you ever think of returning?"

"Yes, I did, but somehow I felt like I wouldn't be welcome. Guilty in a way. Like maybe I had used those people, taken advantage of them."

"How do you know the Browns?"

"I met Mr. Brown at the beginning of November at a meeting. I've run into the two of them several times since. May I sit down?"

"Yes, yes. Unless you would rather join the party."

"I like this private get-together better."

"Then pull up the oversized stool. We can watch the city go to sleep."

All of a sudden Michael sat up straight and said, "Did you drive over?"

"Yes, why?"

"In one of the rooms of this vast apartment sits my luggage. After leaving here I was going to a hotel then make a decision about how I would get to Grand Rapids tomorrow. I've heard about some openings in that vicinity and I was going to see if I could arrange some interviews. Suppose I was to drive you home? If I had the courage, I wanted to stop at the cottage for a visit."

"That last line sounds just like that, a line." Annie sighed, and told him about her aunt and the dog. Then she went on, "I was planning on leaving in the morning anyway. I'd love the company, especially if that person is willing to drive."

Michael interrupted her, "Annie, I am so sorry. I knew nothing about your aunt. The Browns didn't say anything. She didn't know of any connection between us."

They could hear the buzzing of conversation in the other room. Several hours passed, and Annie and Michael fell asleep. As the hour grew late Annie thought she heard the door open and Mrs. Brown say something about two extra guests for breakfast instead of one.

• • •

When they walked into the cottage, Michael asked, "You want me to put my things downstairs, don't you?"

Annie moved to the window and stood with her back to him.

After a minute or two, Michael walked up behind her placing his hands on her shoulders. "Did you hear my question?"

"I don't know what I want, Michael. I'll tell you what, why don't you put them below and I'll get us something to eat."

It got dark early and at 9:00 they each decided to turn in. Annie had to go to work the next day. Michael was going to use her phone and his laptop computer to get things organized and rolling.

Annie wrote in her journal.

> *The Return of Tarzan. What kind of a sequel would it be? Only time would tell. Dream on, woman of the jungle.*

The next days were busy with work. One evening at supper Michael mentioned that he had been over in the woods.

New Year's Eve they snuggled up and watched TV. New Year's Day they went to a movie and ' ate on the way home. Then they stopped by John's and also popped in to surprise Maude.

On January second Michael borrowed Annie's car and went to Grand Rapids for a couple of interviews. On the way out the door, he kissed her and said he was sure he would be back for an early supper.

Early afternoon Annie baked a pie, so it could be served warm. She fussed with the table and even dug around until she found the candle holders and candles.

At 5:00 Annie stopped preparations. She sat in a kitchen chair, folded her hands and waited. She saw the car come down the drive. She held the door open for him to come inside.

"Are you Annie Tucker?"

"Yes."

"Do you know a Michael Hillerman?"

"What happened? Is he in the hospital, officer?"

"I'm afraid he was killed. The roads have turned slippery and a semi truck went out of control on the highway just outside of town."

The dreams, the dreams you have at night when you are falling, tumbling head over heels, falling: and there's no place to land, just open space. That's what was happening. The sickening feeling in your stomach when you gasp for air.

The policeman must have sat her in the chair. She gripped the hard seat with both hands, she couldn't let go. Annie opened her eyes and looked at the young man. He appeared to be of Mexican descent. His look of helplessness is what brought her around. His assigned mission was a frightful one. Too many accidents in the area had forced him to come alone.

Annie made herself stand, and asked him, "May I hold on to your hand for just a few moments? It may help us both get through this. I need to feel the touch of warm human contact. I need to be reassured that there are people still alive in my small universe.

"Please sit down a minute. I have to make a phone call to see how to handle this. If you like, help yourself to a piece of pie. This will take a few minutes." Annie called Chicago, getting hold of Mr. Brown.

"I'll call his folks and get back to you right away."

Annie offered the officer a cup of coffee and sat down with him.

"Could I call someone for you, Miss?"

"No thanks. After you leave I'll contact a neighbor."

Mr. Brown rang back, telling Annie what information the officer would need.

"No, I won't come. How could anyone possibly explain who I was? That would be harder than remaining here. No sense to complicate matters for the family. They will have enough to deal with. Can you handle it at that end? Yes, I'm going to call Rosa and Belle immediately. Good-bye and thank you so very much."

The officer took down the information and departed.

"Belle, it's Annie. Can I come and sleep in your spare room again? I can't stay here. It's a long story but Michael has been here the last few days. He was killed a couple of hours ago out on the highway because of slippery roads."

It was not a night for sleeping. Annie could not make herself go back to the cottage yet. She stayed with the sisters in a subdued state. Mr. Brown got hold of her the next day, telling her that they had explained the circumstances to the Hillermans. Plans were completed, and it was time for her to . . .

"Oh Annie, I wish we were closer so we could help. Mrs. Brown sends her love."

John offered to drive Annie to the dealers to look for a replacement car. She found one the same make but a year older than the one before. She decided that later on she would shop for a new one.

The following morning she went to work. Lottie kept a close eye on her. The middle of the morning Lottie thought of a possible solution to the dilemma.

The next day she approached Annie with the idea. "Why don't you take off for Beaufort? You could stay in my old room. My folks would be delighted. They are gone most of the time anyway. They would be pleased to have someone looking after the place while they are gallivanting around."

Annie stopped what she was doing and looked at her. "I have to try something, don't I? I feel like I'm sinking fast, and yes, I have looked in the mirror lately. I'm downright disgusting to have around. The cottage walls are closing in on me. It's worth a try.

"It seems like I spend a lot of time out of the shop. Maybe you should buy my half. You do most of the work. You should get a larger percentage of the profit."

"Your half is not for sale, girl; nor is your spirit. I know you've been through an awful lot, but with the luck you've had, the only way you can go is up. You've been given a heavy dose of bad." She touched Annie's shoulder reassuringly.

"You haven't allowed yourself time to mourn for what you've lost," said Lottie. "Walk the beach in North Carolina until you drop, then sleep. Repeat that until you feel a smile coming on. Let your heart go through the healing process."

Annie walked up to Lottie and hugged her. "I'm going to make arrangements and leave next week. That should get me there by the first of February. I promise not to come back until I'm my charming self again. Lottie, did I ever tell you . . . You're the greatest."

Between packing, business arrangements, and visiting everyone, it proved to be a hectic week.

One late afternoon Rosa called. "My granddaughter is over and wants to play some board games." She gave the excuse that they needed a fourth person.

"I'm not good at that kind of stuff."

"Oh, come on over."

Annie knew it would be good to do something just for fun. She grudgingly shuffled between the houses, kicking at the snow with her boots. Of all things, they had an ancient Ouija board setting on the table.

It was Annie's turn last. They were all laughing at their silly questions and answers. Annie placed her hands gently on the board, not knowing what she wanted an answer to. In her mind, the board turned to a hazy picture of the woods. Her fingers crept lightly all across the board and returned to a spot she recognized. She jumped up and hurriedly donned her boots and jacket. "I think I know where something is waiting for me." She ran out the door.

She hurried down the back yard and across the Lake Road. After a while she angled into the woods. She identified the area. Circling and crossing back and forth, she felt this had to be the place. If she ventured out of the circle her feet seemed to turn back on their own. She searched the ground carefully. Maybe something was hidden beneath the snow. Then she smiled to herself. No good friend of an Indian would have left a clue behind.

It was beginning to get colder and dark. Maybe she should head back. As she turned, a hawk flew out from the tree above her. There was something. Not on the ground, but carefully tied to a low tree branch with a piece of rawhide. His baseball cap.

Annie untied it. She discovered a piece of paper. It was folded small, wrapped in a plastic bag and tucked in the inside rim. Sitting on a stump she slowly opened it. He had dated it.

> 12/29/94
>
> You see, I had planned to visit you. I was going to present the cap as a consolation. But, instead you presented me with a gift of love. Someday we will walk in these woods together and I will delight in your discovering this token.

The communal gathering place of the deer,

My Dear

Surrounded by protective anthills

Voices traveling in the wind

Voices of love

That only you can hear

Will you find my hiding place?

Where I dreamed of your fair face

And love forever

Love unknown

My Sweet Annie

Annie tucked the note in her pocket and returned to the girls. As the door was opened she held the cap out to Rosa. "Will you keep this for me until I decide what to do with it?"

Her eyes filled with tears and she fled for home. Later that evening she built a kindling fire in the fireplace. Annie drew the note from her pocket and read it one more time. It was private. She would never forget the note. These words were to be seen by no other eyes, for they belonged to her alone. She reached down and placed it in the fire. After the fire burned out, she crawled into the bed and cried herself to sleep.

In the morning she wrote in her journal.

Tarzan is gone. I am going also.

She laid the book on top of the clothes in her suitcase.

One last walk up the pathway along the lake was a must. It was an odd morning. There was no movement of any branches or leaves. Yet, there was this strange noise from below. As she watched, she was able to figure it out. The ice flows had broken into smaller pieces. The soft rolling waves were pushing them toward shore. It created a tinkling sound, like pouring tea over a glass full of chipped ice. "Don't know when I'll see you again, Lake of Mysteries, Lake of Beauty, Lake of Curious Noises. But I promise you, I will return."

Annie went over to call on Rosa and Belle just before leaving. They gave her a stack of prestamped postcards with green yarn tied around them. In the process they reminded her that there used to be penny postcards in their day. They said it gave her no excuse for not keeping them posted. She warned them that they would be the only ones she would drop a line to, so they promised to share.

"Bring me the cap, you two. Adjust it so it fits. I need it for luck. I'm off."

PART TWO

 ## CHAPTER 8

Annie didn't feel like sight-seeing on the way to North Carolina, and she didn't push herself. Sticking with the main highways made it easier for on-and-off gas stations, restrooms, eating places, and motels. Conversation was not what she was seeking. It felt good to get out of the snow country, as well as into a different pace of life.

It also felt good to pull into the driveway of Lottie's parent's home in Beaufort. No one was about, but Annie located the key and let herself in. They had left a note on the table, giving a big welcome and stating that they wouldn't be home for a week or so.

Her first reaction was disappointment. The more she contemplated this, however, the better she liked it. It would give her time to adjust before their return. She'd follow Lottie's instructions, run and rest, run and rest.

Annie sat on the porch a while before unloading the car. Some neighbors waved. They seemed to be expecting her. There was no attempt to rush over and greet her. It appeared that the word was out. ("Let her come to you when she's ready for company.") Annie took a deep breath and began to relax.

She could get reacquainted with the town and surrounding area. She hoped it would produce some results in clear thinking. It wasn't necessary today to look at the future. In the meantime her decision was to unplug her thinking apparatus and just live day by day. She could enjoy life and its beauty and see what developed.

Annie showered and changed, then went to the neighborhood seafood restaurant for supper. Ah, yes, the seafood. Oh, how she savored the dishes from the Atlantic. She wandered down the wooden walkway and in and out of the tourist shops. Annie enjoyed sitting until after dark and watching the lights come on in the town and on the few boats along the dock. It was not overly warm, just pleasant.

When she got back to Lottie's room, she dropped her clothes on the floor and climbed into bed. Annie slept more soundly than she had for months. The sun shining in her face woke her up. She was amazed to discover it was 10:00 a.m. How many years had it been since she had slept in? The day was half over. She unpacked her things and carefully put everything away in drawers and stored her suitcases in the closet. She found an empty spot in the garage and stacked her few boxes inside one another, as best she could. She hiked to the nearest local eating place and put away a big breakfast.

She then walked the area along the shore, investigating everything. She stopped and looked out over the water, realizing that she had put her things away as if to stay awhile. So be it, she decided.

That afternoon she found a supermarket and set in supplies. At least while Lottie's folks were away, she felt comfortable using the kitchen freely and also the laundry area. But she did find out where the Laundromat was located.

It was at this point that she popped her first postcard in the mail. All she did was draw a smiley face on it, and ask Rosa and Belle to call Lottie.

Before the week was out, Annie had taken a job as a waitress at one of the restaurants that bordered the water. She was standing in the neighbors' yard visiting with them as Lottie's parents pulled into the driveway. Even in this short span of time it almost felt as if it was her place and they were coming to visit.

A second card traveled through the mails, this one telling of her job and the return of the homeowners.

Before long she was invited to be a part of the group of young people who worked on the staffs of the various restaurants in the area that arranged social and fun activities. It was for singles only, sort of a group date arrangement. Very seldom was there any real organization. It was just a throw-out-your-idea plan. If you thought of something special you were interested in seeing or doing, you'd find out if you had any cohorts.

• • •

In the spring, someone brought up trail rides out at Cedar Island. Although none of them were riders, the idea appealed to quite a few of them. It took less than an hour to get there. There were beach rides, picnic rides, a dinner meal, and an evening ride. That was great; all the different restaurant shifts could participate.

For Annie, it was a wonderful discovery. At least once a week she traveled the trail out to the horses. Sometimes someone would be going; other times she went by herself. Lottie's folks came and went. The arrangement was perfect. Annie wrote home again.

> *Dear Rosa and Belle, I have come across the animal called the horse. Why was this creature not a part of my life before? My love life is centered on a gentle old soul named Ginger. She is my favorite. We seem to understand each other. Annie*

As summer wore on, Annie strolled around Beaufort. She studied the architecture of the small two-story white houses. If she had written home about her findings she would have titled it: Pillars, Porches, Picket Fences, and Porch Swings.

Oftentimes she walked by them without seeing them at all. It was when she would recall why she had come here. It was then she could still feel the awful hurt inside from the loved ones she had lost. But the thoughts were not occurring as often as they had in the beginning, and that was a relief.

Annie and one of the other waitresses from work, Mary Beth, begged a week off in early August to do a bit of traveling. They stayed overnight in Beaufort, South Carolina, at a fabulous inn. It was just a block from the Intracoastal Waterways.

They were lucky and by chance caught the artist Jackson Causey at his home studio and gallery. The enlightening part was that they were able to talk to him and see his work in progress. His realist paintings of the American scene were wonderful. Each young woman purchased a T-shirt. They pulled them on over what they were wearing so they didn't have to carry them in a bag. One depicted the Whistle Stop Café from Fried Green Tomatoes. The other was the green pick-up truck from The Bridges of Madison County.

When they returned to their room, there was an envelope propped against the lamp near the large overstuffed reading chair. The footstool was as large as the chair itself. There were puffy pillows so one could get comfy. In the envelope was a hand-printed card, welcoming them and encouraging them to enjoy the Inn's Southern Hospitality.

On the way in from shopping, Annie had asked if they could have some coffee in their room. It seemed like a simple request.

A light tap was heard on the door. After the delivery girl left, Annie and Mary Beth giggled like schoolgirls. What a beautiful tray: a coffee pot, cups and saucers, delicate spoons, linen napkins, creamer and sugar dishes. Included was a china plate with dainty cookies. Southern ladies, indeed, they were. And there they stood in their jeans and new T-shirts, snickering like children.

They didn't change their outfits, but they did change their composure. They took on the pose of fine ladies and carried on the suitable conversation, each with her pinkie held in the acceptable position. It took on the air of a children's tea party. It was glorious fun.

In Savannah, Georgia, Annie bought a large postcard, thinking that should excite the girls.

> *Dear Rosa & Belle,*
> *What an interesting city.*
> *Staying in a swell Bed and Breakfast. It used to be a factory that made overalls.*
> *Cobblestone streets at the waterfront. Music along River St. at night. Consuming tons of shrimp. Tell Lottie I spent hours in a candy shop.*
> *Have many innovative ideas.*
> *Annie*

Having abandoned everyday life for freedom and adventure, the young women were intoxicated with laughter. Their compatibility was beyond expectation. There hadn't been much time during working hours to develop close friendships. It was a lark for each of them.

The two girls were ready to get back to work at the restaurant and to their regular routines. Annie dropped Mary Beth off at the apartment that she shared with several of the girls and headed to Lottie's parents' house.

Annie was fascinated with the shrimp boats that traveled the waterways near the Anderson's house. They were on the move around the clock. She watched them unload and heard the voices echoing across the water in the stillness of the night. The lights from the boats twinkled and reflected on the water like tiny Christmas tree lights.

It would be easy to stay in Beaufort, get a place of her own. It was pleasant, easygoing, fun, and required so few responsibilities. But something was lacking. Annie was almost twenty-five, and this wasn't home. Yes, it was time to think seriously of heading home, time to think of the future. She was not sure what it held for her, but now she felt she could handle it.

8/31/95

Rosa & Belle,

Time to start for home.

A few days, a few months?

Things I'd like to do and see.

At this point heading for the Chesapeake Bay area. Later, Annie

Thunder rattled the window, waking Annie like a natural alarm clock. Her Omni was packed; she could be ready in minutes. It was still dark and earlier than she had planned on leaving, but it would enable her to outdistance the commuter traffic.

She ordered at the window of the first fast-food chain she spotted. She devoured the food almost before the rain splats hit the windshield.

Somewhere along Highway 13 she pulled off at a diner and had a tuna salad sandwich and stale potato chips for lunch. After she turned toward Cambridge on Highway 50, the rain let up a bit, but something was wrong. She felt queasy. If the restroom in the diner was an indication of the cleanliness in the kitchen, she suspected that was the trouble.

The original plan had been to take some side roads looking for a cove so she could get some photos early in the morning. Ahead was a village. Through the wipers she saw the sign: Freddie's Motel.

Annie pulled in. Jumping over puddles, she ran inside the office. Hurriedly, she scribbled her name and grabbed the key the man laid on the counter.

Annie moved the car in front of number 6 and made sure she locked the doors so her belongings would be safe. The room was dingy, with frayed mustard-colored drapes.

After that, caution was forgotten. She threw her purse and car keys on the dresser and rushed into the bathroom. So much for tuna fish.

She'd left the bathroom light on but the door pulled closed. The outside light peeking around the closed drapes was enough. She was sweating, hitting the bathroom, cramps, the bathroom, and finally fitful sleep.

Annie heard a tap on the door. Her mind was cloudy. She couldn't remember what she had done with the room key, or if she had turned the lock after entering. Staggering to the door she looked through the peephole. Standing there was a man of enormous size in disheveled clothing.

"You must have the wrong room. Please go away, I'm sick," she pleaded.

Looking down she saw the doorknob begin to turn. With that she began to be aware of what was happening. She reached for the lock but wasn't fast enough, and the door was being pushed open. She wasn't strong enough to stop the movement.

Then she felt the answer to the problem rumbling from her stomach. She whipped the door open and threw up all over the shocked individual. At the same time she shoved him backward, slamming the door and locking it. She could hear him screaming obscenities as he made his way back toward the office.

Annie hit the floor running, snatching a towel, her purse and keys. She ran out, leaving the door wide open. Gravel flew up around the tires as the car skidded sideways.

Returning to Highway 50 and moving on until it connected with 301, her foot began to lift slowly from the accelerator.

She had so wanted to go into St. Michael's, but that was impossible now.

There was a small sign along the highway: Ma's Fine Food, Open 24 Hours, 5 miles ahead. She'd have a look.

Annie pulled into the well-lit parking lot, up close to the building. She turned the ignition off, double-checked to see that the car doors were locked, shook uncontrollably, and collapsed.

When she woke, the stench of vomit and sweat baking in the heat of the enclosed vehicle made her wonder if she was lying in the bottom of a cesspool.

She began shaking again. Soon it would be daybreak. Annie wondered if it would be possible to get inside to the washroom without being conspicuous.

Hurrying past two waitresses, she could imagine what they thought. Annie had her head over the sink trying to clean up when the door swished open.

"One of the girls said she thought the lady in the john needed help."

Annie rose up so that her reflection was in the mirror.

"Well, I'd say so," added the woman.

"Motel . . . Town of Escape . . . Freddie's . . ."

"Freddie figures if a woman is alone she's easy pickin'. Trouble is, there's some big names around there that use the place for different reasons. So not much happens."

"Could I have a pail with soapy water? My car is a mess."

"Clean it, lock it, but leave a window cracked for air. The girls will keep an eye on it. Come in the back door. That's where I hang my hat. I'll lay out stuff for a shower, then you'll feel more human. Just call me Ma."

• • •

Annie let the water run and run. The shampoo smelled like oranges. When Ma returned, Annie was sitting on the davenport drying her hair with a towel. The tattered brown kimono felt like heaven.

"I'll lock any valuables you got in the safe. Then I'll round up a sheet and pillow and you can sleep there."

Annie lowered her head to the pillow and felt the sheet pulled up around her shoulders. Then all the world was quiet.

When she began to wake, she lay there thinking about Ma, large-boned and buxom, with the soft face of an angel and a heart that opened to strangers.

Next to her was an old TV tray with cartoon characters on it, several packets of crackers, and a small dinner bell. She had no more than touched the bell when the door opened. There stood Ma with a big smile.

"Slept the day away, did you? Time for chicken soup?" In between spoonfuls, Annie's story tumbled out.

"Can't send you on your way 'til you're on your feet. Dishwasher's off for a couple of days. How about filling in? I'll pay with room and board."

Two days stretched to two weeks. Two full weeks of learning and leaning. It was hot in the dish room. Annie worked hard, the sweat poured off of her, and the rebuilding poured in. She knew she was being looked after. It was a good down-home family feeling.

Ma reminded her, in many ways, of Aunt Mary. She acted a little tough; maybe you had to appear that way in order to run a business along the highway and survive. But under the exterior of toughness was an individual everyone should experience at least once in a lifetime. A genuine person. There is no question as to this person's love and loyalty. If you realize who you are dealing with, you handle her with great care. For in your hand, you hold something that is irreplaceable.

The girls were fun and foolish, and also had rough edges. Annie had no problem making out the words to the songs blaring out from the country music station. If the place was empty, they all danced around, gyrating in risqué fashion—all of them, including Ma and Annie. It was a wonder they weren't arrested.

Ma came back from town one day with a male cat in tow. She said she'd heard about him on the radio. The Humane Society was broadcasting a plea; they could only promise to keep him one day.

He was a five-toed black cat, with one eye brown and one green. The green eye was the only one that worked. The brown eye was dysfunctional. Ma was delighted that she got there first. The poor thing looked like a truck had backed over him, more than once. But he was as friendly as all get out.

Ma was proud of herself. "Figgered we needed a feller around the place. I've decided to call him Poncho." So, now they didn't have to worry. Poncho would protect them from any ruffians.

 CHAPTER 9

On Sunday the 17th of September, Annie dropped another card in the mail saying she was going to the coast of Maine. She repacked the car, then searched for Ma.

"Where's that safe of yours?"

"Time to go?"

"I'm afraid so."

When Ma came back she handed Annie a shoe box.

"It's freezing cold."

"Can you think of a safer place?"

They both laughed, but the tears were dangerously close to the surface.

"Will you keep in touch?"

Annie turned quickly toward the car, and nodded. She started the engine and waved out the window without looking back.

Annie experienced the horrors of driving through some big cities to see the sights that no citizen should miss. She wished she had missed them all. The pace of these metropolises could drive a saint mad. It took several days to get through the maze and arrive in the area where she really wanted to be.

A card from Maine read:

> *Rosa and Belle,*
> *Experience in Chesapeake area was bad. And*
> *also very good. Tell you when I get there.*
> *Missing you all.*
> *Love, Annie*

Annie stayed in Stonington, Maine, two nights. She poked in every nook and cranny she had time for. She used up many rolls of film. One advantage of being alone was that she didn't have to consider a traveling companion when taking photos. She could just pull the car off the side and hop out. She could sit in wet weeds or roll on her stomach, whatever was required to get just the angle she desired.

The mail boat that left for Isle au Haut carried Annie, along with several other people, out to the island. There Annie spent time crawling on boulders. Her camera wasn't fancy, but it gave her a lot of satisfaction.

The atmosphere was as alluring as a merman. Annie could feel it beckoning to her. She could sense it calling, "Come place your hand in my waters and feel the tensions of life subside." It beckoned her spirit. "Feel the winds that fill the sails of the boats leaving my harbors." There was a mystical aura that hovered in its inlets. It continually murmured promises of the unforeseen future. The coast of Maine would be hard to leave.

One more thing was enticing her. She drove up to Bar Harbor. She had to try to see a whale. The tour she took was usually quite optimistic about locating whales because of special equipment on board. "Off to the left," the man on the mike claimed. Annie's eyes got like saucers.

There . . . There . . . There. There were two of them. Annie could not believe the thrill of the sight of these magnificent creatures. The camera was forgotten on the seat beside her; another momentous occasion not recorded. It didn't matter. To observe a whale with her own eyes was an unforgettable happening.

Nothing on the Great Lakes around her home state of Michigan had prepared Annie for what it would be like to ride the high seas, keeping pace with whales. Lake Michigan could get rough and nasty, but the ocean gave her a feeling of wildness, down deep, trying to break loose.

The ride took all afternoon and, eventually, Annie retrieved her camera and take photos of some seagulls, passing sailboats, and a lighthouse. She smiled to herself when she remembered that she could have taken pictures like these from her own front yard.

The salty sea air spurred Annie's appetite. After returning to the dock, she sought out a quaint restaurant that specialized in lobster and crab. She ate alone inside, but she told the waitress that she wanted to watch the harbor lights for awhile, so she took her after dinner coffee and dessert out on the porch.

Annie traveled some back roads to Michigan. The car window was open, and the warm winds of autumn were blowing in her hair. The effect made her sleepy, so she pulled into a small hotel in western Pennsylvania around 5:00 p.m. She wasn't very hungry, so she bought a package of Pinwheel cookies and a small container of milk from a nearby convenience store. After eating several of the cookies, she took a hot shower and was in bed by 7:30.

At 4:00 a.m. Annie woke feeling fully rested and very hungry. She was on the road by 5:00, keeping a look out for an eatery with lights glowing from the windows.

It was still dark outside. There was a kindergarten moon pasted up there, along with an abundance of sticky stars. She drove for a couple of hours on this clear cool morning. As she came through a small town, she spotted a gentleman walking down the sidewalk. She rolled down her window and asked if there was a place open for breakfast this early. He turned toward her with a big smile, and said, "The Dee-Lite, in the next block, best food in town." He chuckled and walked on in that direction.

On the front of the building, up above the windows, was a papier-mâché potato head. It had a sideways grin, and sunglasses pushed up toward the forehead. Annie stepped inside. It seemed to be a friendly place. On the front of the menu it read:

Our Famous Specialty
The Original Farmer's Breakfast: eggs, fried potatoes, ham, onion and green pepper

She decided to give it a try. She'd order the smaller size. The man next to her ordered the same. The waitress asked, "What kind of toast do you want?"

His reply was, "Whatever kind is easy to remember when you go to put the order in." That drew a chuckle all around. All the patrons seemed to be familiar with one another. In fact, someone came through the door and one of the men who was leaving said, "Good morning, family."

The man Annie had asked directions from walked in, removed his coat, and proceeded to fill coffee cups, greeting everyone. Then he came and sat down next to her at the counter.

She gave him a smirky smile and said, "Pretty sneaky. I take it it's your place?"

He laughed and they talked for quite a while. He was excited about a quick trip to Paris in a couple of days. He owned a place in Belize. His business interests were many. Annie explained where she had been and where she was headed.

"Actually, I learned how to cook in France," the man explained.

Annie looked amazed. You mean . . . you mean you attended the Cordon Bleu School?"

"Oh, no, no," the man said with a laugh. "I was a cook with Patton's Armor Corps during World War Two. I got all the training I needed on how to cook massive amounts of eggs, bacon, biscuits, and coffee. After the war, I came home and put that training to use. I opened this café and I'm still feeding an army . . . smaller, perhaps, but just as hungry and just as ugly."

Across the room a voice said, "Don't you believe a word of it."

The men sitting nearby slapped the table in rowdy agreement. Everyone laughed. The coffee pot was passed around again and Annie dallied awhile, listening to local gossip and arguments about the weather.

Time after time Annie saw a waitress walk up to a table and ask, "The usual?"

After the owner finished his second cup of coffee, he turned to her again. "I was pulling your leg about the cooking. That's why the statement got such a roaring laugh. When I was in the service I was a survival training instructor. You need that to run a restaurant too."

"So, this is like a second family?"

"Yes, it is. Each table has a different story. That group of ladies at the big round table in the front: they go for a walk each weekday, then gather here for breakfast. They exchange books, and share pictures of trips and grandkids.

"The man over there, eating his oatmeal, and reading a book on motivation?"

"Yeah."

"He's in office supplies. As soon as he opens the store this morning; he leaves for Philadelphia for a meeting.

"I'm glad you stopped today. See the poster on the wall?"

"Yes."

"Our yearly party is tonight. We do it as a celebration of another successful year. It's at my place. Everyone is welcome, our regular customers and someone like yourself, just passing through. The details are all there. Lots of shrimp and other good things to eat."

"It sounds great. But I've had all the shrimp I can eat for a while. This is your second family; it makes me long to put the miles behind me and get back to my family. Thanks, anyway."

As she later headed out of town, she thought about the café owner. Life was full of interesting people and she had a lot of them to meet yet. Time to get on with it. She was trying to complete the clearing of her mind, to allow the final freeing of her soul and lifting of the last of the burdens from her heart.

A gypsy she wasn't. She formed attachments to people and places too easily. She wanted to gather them and take them with her. It would have been easier to stay than to move on. But the ribbon attached to Annie's heart was pulling her homeward. No place in the world was more beautiful than Michigan during the autumn. She needed to get back.

Part Three

 ## Chapter 10

Just before dark the Omni pulled into the cottage driveway. Annie was glad she hadn't seen anyone as she had passed the houses on Maude's View. She had driven hard that last day and was exhausted. Once she got close, the homing pigeon instinct seemed to click in. No matter how weary she was, there was no stopping.

Before taking her belongings inside, she went out and sat on the ground overlooking Lake Michigan. Her heart picked up a beat. Placing her hands flat on the earth on each side of her, Annie was sure she could feel a pulse beneath the first fall of the leaves. This was home. This was where she belonged. It was as if the soil and the water were sending a message: "Welcome home, Annie Tucker."

Annie smiled as she walked toward the back door. She unlocked it and stepped inside. It was dusty, but other than that everything was as it should be. She moved her things from the car. Tomorrow she would put everything away and give the place a quick once-over. It would be necessary to restock the shelves, refrigerator, and freezer.

She glanced at the calendar setting on the desk: January 1995. Annie flipped through the months, leaving the October pages open. Here we go again.

The phone rang and she jumped. She'd never had it turned off, thinking she would return in days, not months. "Hello."

"It is you, Annie. I was alarmed when I saw the cottage lights. I thought I would at least startle whoever was there if I rang in."

"Rosa, it's good to hear your voice."

"Will you come for breakfast in the morning? We must talk."

"Sounds great. I'll see you then." Annie was sorry she had been abrupt. She had a strange feeling something was wrong. There had been a disturbing tone to Rosa's voice. She'd find out.

Before first light Annie was awakened from a sound sleep. Sitting up straight in bed she heard a terrible noise. It sounded like a wild elephant gone mad and trumpeting through the underbrush. Then she recognized the noise. All those months and they still hadn't repaired the brakes on the garbage truck. She dropped back to the pillow and drifted off to sleep for another hour or so.

* * *

Annie made up her grocery list and was knocking on Rosa and Belle's door by 8:00 a.m. Rosa let her in. Something was the matter. Annie stood in the doorway and stared at Rosa. She looked okay, but still . . . What was it? Annie whipped her head around, taking in everything in the room. "Belle. Where is she?"

"She's gone, Annie." Rosa's face seemed to shatter, and she crumpled into a kitchen chair.

"What are you telling me?"

"She got pneumonia a few weeks after you left."

"Oh, my dear Rosa, you knew I was at Lottie's parents. You should have said something last night. I'd have come right over."

"In either case, you couldn't have helped. We talked about it, and decided you had enough to work through."

"My dear sweet Rosa. You have helped me so often and I wasn't here to help you." Annie was on her knees by Rosa's chair. She laid her head in her lap. "Dear Rosa, sometimes you must think of yourself. I should have been here for you."

"I'm just glad you are back, Annie. I've missed you and your cheerful outlook. The postcards have helped to keep me going. We all want the best for you, Annie. I guess each of us thinks of you as our special girl."

Annie shook her head. "You are all doing your part, but I haven't been fulfilling mine. I've thought about myself long enough. It's time for me, and everyone, to get back on track."

"Actually, I've done quite well. Would it have helped had I gone away the way you did?"

"Running doesn't help; it's just a different way of handling it. Mourning is something that has to work its way through your system. There were times when it was physically painful, and I would feel so strange I would wonder what was the matter with me.

"Mentally, emotionally, it rips you apart some days. It doesn't matter where you are or what you're doing. Manufacturers design all different kinds of running shoes, but none that let you escape the reactions of death. It's impossible to run fast or far enough.

"There were times when the world seemed lifeless. I got the feeling it had closed its doors to me. I was barely functioning, outside looking in, and caring little. When someone you love dies, you perish a little yourself, down deep.

"It would be easier to hide down there than to struggle back to the surface of life. It's like some monster is stalking you, wanting to devour you. It takes strength to overpower him."

"How do you do that?" asked Rosa.

"You stand up straight, walk right up and look him in the eye, and smile. He will melt, like the Wicked Witch of the West. Have you been walking the lake path?"

"Not with any spirit."

"Tomorrow morning I'll be by at seven. We'll give each other a boost. We'll begin by thinking of tomorrow, not yesterday. Every time we feel sad, we'll sing a limerick. We may well become the best song and dance team of the era."

"I feel better already, Annie."

"Me, too. You see, we each have a purpose now." They finished preparing the breakfast together. As they sat and drank their coffee Rosa related a sad tale. She told Annie of Belle's last days.

"You see, Annie, Belle used to be a take-charge person, and a fairly pleasant one at that. As I told you once before, a couple of years ago she turned sour on life. I never attributed it to anything special. When you collapsed at John's that time, she reverted back toward her old self. So, you got to know her as she used to be. I was so happy about that."

Rosa sighed deeply before continuing.

"She was always complaining about everything. It didn't register at the time that most of her complaints centered on John. She would make cutting remarks.

"She would draw attention to his white cotton socks and heavy work shoes, and the fact that he wore them when he was even spruced up. I guess he's had trouble with his feet for years.

"He had purchased the property, down the way, and invested lots of time and energy in it before he found out Belle lived on the same road.

"As the end drew near, she called me into her room one afternoon. It was then that she told me of the secret she had carried with her all these years. It seems that John had wanted desperately to marry Belle when she was young, even though he was three years younger than she. He had asked our father for her hand. Papa knew the type of man John was and was pleased for her. When John came to propose marriage, she was embarrassed and laughed at him. What would people think? He was crushed.

"At that point he went on to school to study animal husbandry, and devoted his life to that. Later, she did become interested in him, but he stayed clear of her. No one wants to get hurt like that again. She was lonely. But she was sure people would think she was chasing after him, what with him being younger and her not married yet.

"When I walked into the funeral John was sitting in the back row. He was bent over with his head in his hands, his body was shaking with grief. I put my arm around his shoulder. He looked up at me and said, 'I've loved her all these years.'"

Rosa paused a moment, reviewing the scene in her mind.

"I told him she had confided in me. Just days before, how she had loved him also, and how she had admired what he had become. I asked if he had been up front to view her body and he shook his head no. I took his arm and we walked together to say our last good-byes. I continued to hold his arm and insisted he sit with the family, where he had belonged for years. Pride can be so destructive.

"We have bolstered each other up these past months, and I have become very fond of him."

Annie was in tears. "One piece of advice: If he is also fond of you, do not let pride ruin things twice in your family."

"But we would feel unfaithful to Belle."

"Hogwash! That's what I mean. If there are feelings between you both and you don't deal with them as you should, you'll both have to answer to me. I must go. I haven't called Lottie yet."

"John is unhappy with you. He expected to hear from you because of your strong friendship. He knew you were only going to write to Belle and me, but he hoped you would break your rule."

"Well, I better get on down there and make amends. I must warn you, if you don't snatch him up, I'm going to put him on my list of probables."

Rosa smiled and flashed an OK sign with her finger and thumb. Annie let herself out.

Annie walked to John's. She didn't call out, but searched for him. Spotting him in what he called his "shed," she stood silently in the doorway and watched him work. When he turned and was aware of her, they moved toward each other and into a big embrace.

She stepped back and looked at him. They were each smiling, but their eyes were full of tears. "No, John, we mustn't cry. I have just come from Rosa's and I have used up my allotment of tears for today."

He sat on a stool and motioned for her to sit on another one across from him. Then the smiles broke out in full force. They talked and laughed. She claimed it was good to be home, and he claimed how good it was to have her there.

She stepped in at Maude's before returning home. When she walked in she was delighted to find her doing the dishes with her walker handy. "So, what's new?"

"Well, you weren't around to entertain me, so I've been taking some adult education classes for fun. I've also been going to the hospital once a week doing therapy. Also, I go there once in a while as a volunteer."

"Boy, it's going to be hard to keep up with you now."

"You're darn right."

Annie gave Maude a digest version of all the travel news she had shared in detail with John. Maude brought up the subject of Belle's death and shared a few memories about her. Tea was served and they sipped and talked, but Annie excused herself, explaining she needed to check with her business partner.

Annie arrived home in great spirits. She dialed the store number, and Lottie answered. She wanted to think of something clever to say. Instead, all she could come up with was, "Guess who?"

"Why, it's that old rascal Annie. Get yourself down here so I can have a good look at you. I thought you probably fell in a vat of milk chocolate in Savannah. In fact, I've been watching the catalogs to see if they came out with something life-sized. I'd order it, and when it was delivered, I'd carefully melt the outside away and there you would be."

"Cut the dribble. What's happening down there?"

"Come and see. And, Annie, I've found me a fella, and I'm going to be married."

"My gosh, I can't leave you alone a minute. I'll be right there. First, I want to hear all about this marriage business. Then we'll talk store."

The two of them were going crazy trying to wait on customers while also trying to catch up on everything at the same time.

"How's Kate? And the Tea Room?"

"Great! I think she's enjoying it now. She's got her pattern worked out, and she's more relaxed."

The hours passed quickly. After the door was locked, a tall nice-looking young man rapped lightly on the window. Annie watched her exuberant college friend transform into a woman before her eyes. The change made Annie yearn to be loved by someone special, too.

What a day. Annie was worn out, not having planned on seeing everyone her first day back. She had completely forgotten to stop and get any groceries. She found a can of soup, and had a few Pinwheels left from her trip home.

One more thing, then she could wrap it up for today. She got a tablet out of the desk and wrote to Lottie's folks. She also compiled a letter to Ma, inquiring about Poncho and the girls.

She had told her stories to each person she had shared the day with, skipping the detail about Freddie's. As she sat composing the letters, she went into greater depth to let these people know what they had meant to her growth and how they had touched her heart.

 CHAPTER 11

The morning walk with Rosa became a ritual. Annie could not believe the monstrous new house being constructed next to the Browns. While she was away the one that had stood there for years had been completely removed. The new house made the homes around it look like Monopoly pieces. Rosa said that there was only one thing she found encouraging about it. The family that was having it built: the mother spent time with the children drawing colored chalk pictures on the driveway. So, they couldn't be all bad. Rosa and Annie hoped they would get invited in once it was completed. It would have to be spectacular. They wondered if these people would be comfortable visiting in their homes. Time would provide the answers.

Rosa told of the writer who rented the small A-frame for a spell. A personable fellow, she felt. "You would have enjoyed talking with him, Annie. He walked every day, too.

"The larger A-frame was rented for several months by a strange family. The grandmother came to visit. Everyone had called her the umbrella lady. No matter what the weather, she was out, with the umbrella. Then one day they were gone, sort of a disappearing act. Maude watched the sky to see if 'Grandma Poppin' was about. It was an odd situation. And we can't have any odd folks living on our street, can we?" With that, they laughed and joined arms.

Those who lived here full time wished there were not so many rentals on the short street. But it did manage to keep things lively. Still, the long-timers seemed to keep things hopping without the additional help.

• • •

Frank glanced up from his computer equipment and out the side window. Immediately, he was transfixed. The house next door, which had been empty the whole time he had been in residence, suddenly had a forest nymph in the yard. She was a pretty little thing, pageboy haircut, old jeans, and a T-shirt with something written across the front.

It looked as if she had come out with intentions of raking some leaves. Instead, she proceeded to dance around the yard, as if her spirit had just been set free.

Frank went from window to window following her graceful movements. He stepped onto the porch and into the yard. Although she didn't seem aware of his existence, he felt compelled to walk toward her. As he drew closer he saw the tape player and heard the smooth country music. It was a nice tape. A different melody started playing.

Suddenly she turned, as if expecting him, held her arms in dance position and asked, "Do you waltz?"

"Yes."

"It's 'Bluegrass Fiddler,' my favorite." She closed her eyes. They danced through the leaves in the uneven yard as though they were dancing at a cotillion. The expression on her face told that she was elsewhere. Frank wondered where. He wished he was there with her, to be her only partner.

The music came to an end. She withdrew her hands and stood still, looking off in the distance. He could not take his eyes off her. She shook her head, as if to come awake. Looking at him, she smiled. Her eyelids then were lowered and she appeared shy.

She made a face and said, "I do hope you don't have a wife peeking from a window nearby. If so, she will have an instant dislike for me. We were not dancing together as strangers."

He had not wanted to take his arm from her waist. She was right; they had danced this soft waltz like lovers. He took a step back. "No wife."

It was at that moment that they were attacked by a rowdy Golden Retriever pup. He wanted to play and almost knocked them over.

In unison they said, "Does he belong to you?" Frank said, "I've never seen him before, and I've been here several months."

"Where is here?"

"There, next door."

Annie sat down in the leaves and played with the dog. "Have a chair," she said, as she pointed at the ground. "Looks like he's ten or twelve weeks old, and full of that kind of energy. I hope he wasn't dropped. I'll check it out. So, the Browns decided to rent the place out?"

"No, it's mine. They didn't feel up to the moving back and forth anymore. The Browns are my aunt and uncle. When I heard they were thinking of selling, I contacted them immediately. By the way I haven't introduced myself: Frank E. King."

"Frankie King: sounds like a rock star." Annie rolled on the ground, with the pup, laughing at what she had said.

Frank brushed his pants off and started to walk over to his place. "Just for that I won't help you up."

Annie laughed harder than before. "Nice meetin' you, neighbor. I'm called Annie Tucker."

Frank turned back. "Not Tucker like in trucking, and Tuckerville and all that?"

"Yep."

"Gosh, our families have been doing business for several years."

"What kind of business?"

"Office equipment."

"Oh, sure, the King Company, out of Chicago."

"I was tired of the big city. It was an excellent opportunity to expand further into Michigan. I'm running the new branch office out of a room in the house, at this point. It's got a tricky name: Complete Computer Sales, Supplies, and Service."

"You're right, that's some name."

"If I were to run a contest to come up with a better one, you'd probably be mad if you didn't win."

Annie wasn't sure how to take that remark. "There's no question as to what you do. Maybe that is best." Then she decided to give him a nudge in return. "Good! Now that you are close, you can give us better service at Lottieannie's."

He picked up on it, but made no comeback. "I'm on the road some, so I won't be in your way." With that he turned and headed home for the second time.

Just loud enough, he could hear Annie make one more comment. "Mighty fine lookin' boots, neighbor."

She picked up the squirming dog and went in to use the phone. Calling every conceivable source was of no avail. "Well, Lad, you are stuck here with me tonight. I'll check more thoroughly tomorrow." Annie had made it to the grocery that day but had nothing available for dog food. She searched through the cupboards for something that would fill a puppy's tummy for one night. She found some Vienna sausages. Then she plopped down into an easy chair.

The pup cocked his head one way then the other. "Well, kiddo, if you are all alone, how about us being alone together?" He struggled up on her lap and went to sleep. *Hope he doesn't belong to anyone. We could be good pals,* she thought, as she stroked his head.

Just before nodding off, Annie reviewed the picture of her new neighbor. He was about 5 feet 6 inches, 160 pounds, high forehead, brown hair brushed back, slender face, pleasant smile, azure blue eyes. He had worn a flannel shirt, with cuffs rolled partway, and nice jeans. And she really was impressed with those cowboy boots. It seemed as though thing had started off really nice, then they were stepping on each others' toes, and she wasn't sure why.

The following day she checked the paper and called the radio station as the last resort. Poor little pup, guess no one loves him, except me. Annie scooped him up and gave him a hug. "Well Lad, it's you and me." She sat down at the desk and read back through her journal, starting in January. Lad curled up by her feet.

Annie was planning ongoing to the civic center, to pick up some apples at the farmer's market. She had called Maude and Rosa, but each was busy. So, she went by herself. The stalls were full of squash and dried flowers. There was one stall she remembered from the previous year. Its owner had corn shocks and pumpkins. The display was very pleasing to the eye. She had taken a picture of it last fall. Running into people was half the appeal of the market. It was her lucky day. She was able to talk to many old friends.

Annie caught sight of Frank and John at the other end, purchasing some mum plants. They looked up and waved.

Later that afternoon Frank was out working in the yard and transplanting his flowers. Annie strolled over with Lad.

"Well, I guess he's your dog. You've got him on a leash. Looks like he's had a bath, too."

"Had the vet look him over and give him his shots. So, he's on the record: I'll call and make his appointment for surgery in six months. Have to start his training now, on simple things." Annie sauntered off to take Lad for his walk.

Annie was raking leaves a couple of days later when Frank started up his truck, then pulled up by where she was working. He leaned over and rolled the window down on the passenger side. "I'm going to town, not Tuckerville but to the north. You need anything?"

"Hey, could I bum a ride? I have a couple of things I have to do up there. I'll buy lunch."

"It's a deal. I don't want to be gone long."

"Me either. I'll get my purse and jacket." As they pulled out of the yard and onto the road, Annie remarked, "I heard on the radio this morning that, in some area, you can order Girl Scout cookies on the Internet. That's awful. Spoils the whole effect. Pretty soon people aren't going to communicate face to face. Nothing against your machines, it just seems kind of sad."

As they rounded the curve, Annie gasped. "What is that?"

"Holly's Landing."

"No, you don't understand. That is not the Holly's Landing I know."

"I've been told someone new purchased the property. They took down the old building and put up this nice facility."

"It used to be just an old place: gas, necessary groceries, a counter and a few stools, ice cream, papers. Sort of a gathering spot."

"Now it's gas, groceries, lottery tickets, and in the back a nice little restaurant. It's an attractive building, and it fits in well with the surroundings. There're a few boat docks. I guess they were there before, but now they're safe and substantial."

When they reached town they separated, agreeing to meet back at the truck in less than an hour. They did, and then it was time for food.

Annie said, "Follow me. We've got to walk two different ways to get lunch." At the waterfront they first turned left and walked up to a very tiny wooden structure. "Four Pronto Dogs and two pops, please." There was a notice tacked up by the register: "LAST DAY 'TIL SPRING." They sat on the grass and watched a few small boats pass by. Annie asked Frank about his family. He filled in a few details, but mostly he sat chewing his food.

Then Annie jumped up and grabbed Frank's hand and said, "Come on, we have to go the other way for dessert." It was one of those cookie shops. "Let us have four of those with the big chunks of chocolate and pecans." Annie took a deep breath. "I bet if you packaged up the smells from this place you could sell that, too. I'm suggesting a new market here. Listen up. It's a money maker for sure." They ate the cookies on the walk back to the truck. On the ride home, Annie talked a little about Aunt Mary, Lass, and Belle, but not about Michael.

Frank pulled up by his house, and Annie hopped out. "Thanks for the lift."

"Thank you for lunch."

Annie hurried home to take Lad out. She and the dog walked over to Rosa's. "Rosa, what's with Holly's Landing?"

Rosa laughed and said, "We've been so busy catching up, I forgot to tell you about that. Next time you're free for lunch we'll have to drive down so you can meet Pierre."

"Is he the new owner?"

"Owner and chef."

"Chef, as in cooking? Boy, we are getting pretty high-class around here."

A few days passed, and it was on the agenda. Rosa and Annie seated themselves in the very attractive dining area. The restaurant appeared to be a separate entity from the rest of the establishment. A waitress took their order.

It wasn't long before a slightly built gentleman, fully attired in chef's whites, complete with the tall pleated hat, backed through the kitchen door. As he turned to walk toward their table Annie tried very hard not to smile. There was no way to deny the fact that he was Chinese.

Rosa proceeded with the introduction. By this time Annie could control herself no longer. Beaming from ear to ear she questioned, "You are called Pierre?"

There was a bow, so slight it was almost unnoticeable. "Yes, missy."

"Are you always so formal?"

"No," and he, too, grinned.

"So, pull up a chair and tell me about yourself. We are your only customers at the moment." Rosa and Annie began to eat. "Why Pierre?"

"I am many people inside with many different ideas. But the name of a French chef is good for business. I have many abilities and thoughts, but business is business. I wished for something small that I could handle myself, with little extra help. This has proved to be very satisfactory. I find happiness here."

The smile that had covered Annie's face turned to a thoughtful look. "I'm happy you've joined our little community, Pierre. A fine chef, indeed, no matter what name you travel under."

There was work at the bakery, and in the yard, then Annie had another free day. She rose early and climbed down the steps to the beach. She rested on the remains of a tree trunk not far from her beach storage building. Her mind was wandering as she lazily looked out at the water and cloudless sky.

She turned and was going to get up and walk along the edge of the water, but she did not stir. In the distance, a figure was moving toward her. It was not a jogger: the stride was different, comfortable, perfect timing. It was an easy pace, but he was covering a lot of ground. His long dark hair was flowing behind. Annie felt as if she had ceased to breathe. She waited. He stopped very close to her. Although he had run quite a distance there was no shortage of breath.

They remained silent, intently looking into each other's eyes. He gently raised his left hand, palm toward her, fingers spread apart. She softly put her right hand up to match his. Their eyes never faltering, they resembled statues.

Then his voice broke the silence of the clear morning. "You are Annie Tucker."

Annie took a deep breath. "And you are Michael's Indian friend."

He took her hand and gently lowered her back onto the tree trunk, then sat beside her.

"How did you find me, and why?"

"I know about you from Michael. Piecing the puzzle together has not been easy. But the meeting had to come about. Something is unfinished. I feel his presence here. I heard that you did not attend his laying to rest. I was away on business at the time and received the information too late. We were more than friends, closer than brothers." With this he raised his face to the sky.

There were two people observing this momentous meeting on the beach. Each of them gathered a different interpretation.

One moved her wheelchair back from the window, feeling it was a private moment that should not be observed. The other watched with a sadness in his heart and went back inside to his work.

When the Indian looked back at Annie, the deep hurt of his loss shown in those dark eyes. She hurt for him, and for herself. Annie asked him to come to the house. He nodded and got up. Lad greeted the stranger as an old friend.

They settled in and began to talk. So much to learn, so much to share. His name was Joe Silvers. He and Michael had met at the university. Their last three years at school they had roomed together.

"He was one of the nicest human beings I have ever known. We were from different worlds. We never dealt with it negatively, but used it as a learning tool. Because of it, each of us grew immensely. It never entered our minds that we would not be in each other's lives until the end of our time. The loss leaves an emptiness in my soul."

"Tell me more about yourself."

Joe continued with his story. "I took business classes in school. At a very young age my father began to teach me the craft of the construction of a wooden canoe. My goal was to have the ability to sell them to the right people.

"I have a lovely wife, Snow. Michael stopped on his way home from here, a year ago, to celebrate the birth of our son, Joey Michael. We live in the U.P. I work for the County Road Commission, part-time on maintaining roads, and I drive the big plows in the winter."

Joe patted Lad's head. "I don't want to forget Hiller. He's my constant companion. I'm not sure what breed of dog he is. Originally, I named him that because of Michael, but he's earned his name. There's nothing he likes better than running in the hills. He was a gift from Michael when I graduated with honors.

"You do not have to tell me your story, Annie, because Michael could speak of nothing else on his last visit. He referred to you as 'His Lady of the Michigan Waters.' He had fallen in love with you."

With that Annie broke down and cried, with no shame, in front of this stranger and friend.

"How did you get here, Joe?"

"I found John's place and talked to him. Then I went back and parked my truck at the Landing. I knew Michael had run the beach from there. I could feel him guiding my footsteps. I think he wanted us to know one another. Now his mission is complete and we can allow him to depart from us and rest in peace."

Annie excused herself. When she returned she handed Michael's cap to Joe. He sat with it in his hands for a long time. "We each got one when we had our first class together at the university. I don't know what happened to mine." He looked down at it, as if remembering many times past. "It had become a part of him. He wore this when he stopped that last time."

"He left it in the woods for me, tied to a limb with a piece of rawhide. There was a note fastened to the inside rim. I would like you to have the cap."

Joe held it tightly. "It is adjusted to a small size."

"I wore it while I was away, for luck."

Joe moved the strap over and put it on his head. "I shall wear it, for with it goes the luck of two of my closest friends. I must go now."

Annie drove him to Holly's Landing. They promised to keep in touch. She walked him to his truck.

It was then that he told her. "I have a gift for you, but you must come before the snow fall and pick it up. Michael had ordered a canoe. He paid for it in advance. Because it was built with the love from my heart, it is very beautiful. The design created by the different woods is almost magical. Michael and I want you to have it. Maybe you can visit the swans again."

Annie burst into tears and Joe held her close. They did not part until she had stopped crying. Then she said, so quietly that he could barely hear, "I'll get John to bring me. I'll contact you."

Annie walked to her car with her shoulders stooped, wondering about what had happened this day. It was a year to the day of her first knowledge of the existence of a man called Michael Hillerman. His moccasins had entered her life. Annie would not want his footprints to be obliterated.

The canoe would be a long-lasting memory of a life that was not allowed to develop fully. It would also be her guide out of the shallows and back into the main stream.

 Chapter 12

Annie sat at her desk and wrote in the journal: Indian Joe. Her hand was lifeless, the pen immovable. She closed the book. She remained there until finally Lad came up by the chair and rested his paw on the leg of her jeans. She started to pet his head and thought, That's why I have you, my little friend, to keep me all in one piece.

Maude called her the next evening after dark. "Annie I'd like you to come over. Don't bring a flashlight. The house will be dark. Just come on in. I'll explain when you get here." Before Annie left she opened the journal and wrote, Maude's Mystery.

Annie opened the door. She felt like she was entering illegally. It seemed appropriate to whisper, "Maude?"

"In the living room."

Annie tiptoed in, and again whispered, "Is this spy stuff?"

Maude chuckled. "I guess there's no reason to whisper. Look through these glasses and tell me what you see."

Annie took the glasses from Maude's hand and scanned the water. "Good grief, Maude, where did you get these?"

"I ordered them from a public safety equipment magazine. They are night vision, infrared field glasses."

"Just like in the movies. What am I looking for? Wait, I see a small light. A boat: maybe . . . 23 feet . . . looks like a . . . Sea Ray. There's a name . . . an S . . . at the end a J. Can't make out the middle. Hold it. Another boat, from out of nowhere. A bigger boat, with no light. Several people. Looks like they are moving something from one boat to the other. Big boat disappeared, just like that. Now the smaller one had moved away also."

"Both are gone, for sure?" Annie nodded. "Hit the lights and come in to the dining room table." Maude got some papers out of a drawer in the china cabinet. "I've made some charts, with dates, times and actions.

"This started back in early spring. I had turned out the lights and was going to turn on my favorite weekly TV show when I noticed a tiny flash of light. It was on the water, and it was still really cold out. My first thought was a plane down, or someone in big trouble."

"What did you do?" asked Annie.

"Well, I got my old binoculars to see what I was dealing with before calling for help. They seem to be out a little over a quarter of a mile, I'd say. I got the same picture you described. So, I talked to a friend, giving him a cock-and-bull story about why I wanted these powerful glasses. I'm just crazy enough that he fell for it.

"Now this has replaced my favorite TV show. It's basically the same action, over and over. That's when I came up with the chart idea. The day of the week and the time never vary, as you can see by the record. I've checked other nights but see nothing. Luckily, the moon was full and no clouds. If it's foggy or cloudy you can't see them. It was also more difficult in the boating season. But now it's cold again and the show is still on."

"This is weird," said Annie.

"There's lots of funny things going on these days. I felt I should report it: but I wanted someone to back me up, someone I could trust. Sometimes the boats come together but you don't see any activity. Could be drug smugglers, espionage; who knows?"

Annie sat there mulling it over. Finally, she spoke. "I'd like to laugh at you, and say you are silly. I'd like to say you read too many books, and watch too many movies on your VCR. But maybe that's why so many bad things happen in the world: everyone turns away, and says forget it."

"Will you come back next week? We'll check it out, then decide whether to take any action."

"One more week. Then we either make a move or forget it and turn the TV back on. It's a deal."

• • •

John heard a knock on his door one afternoon. He was surprised when he opened it to see Frank standing there.

"Come on in, I was about to pour myself a cup of coffee. Will you join me?" Frank made no reply, but John set a cup in front of him anyway. John sipped his coffee, and waited patiently. Frank's mind seemed to be elsewhere.

Finally, the younger man blurted out, "Annie Tucker, do you know much about her?"

John sat back in his chair. So, that was it. "Quite a bit, yes."

"I have known lots of girls, but to tell the truth I felt more challenged and attracted to the computers. I've found women either pushy or boring."

John brought his hand up to his mouth trying to cover his giveaway smile. This fine young man was asking an old bachelor for advice. Maybe another swallow of coffee would slow down the urge to laugh.

"The other day Annie met someone on the beach. Long dark hair, almost looked like an Indian."

So, that was the crux of the thing. "He is an Indian. Silvers. Him and his wife and child live in the Upper Peninsula. He came to see Annie; they had a very close mutual friend who was killed in a car accident here last January. That was one of the reasons Annie was away. In one month's time she lost three friends she was very close to. There was her aunt, the family dog, and Michael. She had difficulty dealing with it all."

"Oh." Frank got up, and walked out the door toward home. He had never raised the cup to his lips.

John leaned against the door frame. Had someone come to lay claim on Annie's heart?

• • •

The week passed and Annie returned to Maude's.

"Annie, did you know I never would have seen the boats if I had been at the water level. Even a small wave would have hidden them. I'm glad I live on this hill. I bet they have programmed 800 trunking phones. Then they can talk to anyone, anywhere, without interference."

"Maude, where do you get this information?"

"I ask questions that are far removed from the subject but that give me the correct answers."

"And people think you are crazy. You are clever and underhanded. There they are! I'm after that name tonight. Big S . . . little letters . . . a . . . 1 . . . 1 . . . y . . . and a capital J. Sally J. Maude, what are you doing?"

"Didn't you ever see anyone try and do cartwheels in a wheelchair? That's what I made out, the Sally J. I'm not crazy!"

The following morning, a twenty-five-year-old woman and an older woman in a wheelchair were entering the office of the Coast Guard in a town north of their homes. A polite young man asked if he could be of assistance.

Annie tried to explain simply that they wanted to report a possible disturbance on the big lake. She got her words tangled, finally prompting the young man to escort them to a private office.

An important-looking, in-charge type of person entered. Accompanying him was a young man, carrying a few papers. He shuffled, reshuffled, and pretended to do some filing, all the while Maude and Annie were relating their story. They were being handled with the thank-you-for-being-alert-citizens routine.

That was before Maude got sick of the patronage program. She let a grenade roll across the floor, in the form of a comment. "I have charted accurate records of these events and one of the boats is the Sally J." The paper shuffler lost control of his papers and they scattered across the room. The change of body language of the important person was amazing.

The latter gained control first. "Thank you so much for reporting this, ladies. We shall certainly look into it. Now, you go home and forget all about it." He assured them they would take care of the matter, as he graciously hurried them out the door.

The office routine continued as they moved through the first set of doors on the way outside. Then all hell broke loose. The man who had questioned them came charging through that door and people were scurrying every which way.

Annie looked at Maude and said, "Let's get out of here." On the way home Annie said, "I don't know if what we did was right or wrong. Maybe we observed something that we shouldn't have. I doubt if we will see any more lights. I think it's best if we forget the whole thing. We did what we thought was best. But here and now I make a declaration: no more of this. We must go back to being plain old Maude and Annie, citizens at rest."

And forget the whole thing they did. Or did they. They never mentioned it again, but each had an imaginative mind. Sometimes late at night if they couldn't sleep they created their own exciting thoughts.

The men on those boats had the hearts of pirates. They were handsome in a rough way, daring and smart. Each of them would return home—one to a woman named Maude, and one to a younger woman by the name of Annie. Whatever it was that they moved from one small craft to another, it was for a good cause. It was never guns or white powder in plastic bags or stolen government secrets. No indeed.

It wasn't long before those boats drifted silently away. Ah yes, it was fun while it lasted. All that remained of the adventure was a rare smile and a twinkle of an eye. It was a hoot for sure.

• • •

The thought crossed Annie's mind that possibly Lottie's coming marriage would affect her involvement in the business venture. If so, would they need to sell? Annie decided if it came to that, she would purchase Lottie's half and search for a dependable manager. It wouldn't be the same, but Annie felt she needed the responsibility it forced on her. Lottie loved it because she had the freedom of full reign. Still, Annie's ideas and business sense were important, too. It had proved to be an incredible partnership. Something you just wish didn't have to change. Annie hoped she was worrying about something she wouldn't have to be concerned about in the end.

Moneywise, Annie knew she was fortunate to have free time. She had the rare privilege of not having to make every penny count for her survival. She also thoroughly enjoyed the busy days at the store. The business was getting hard to control, and they often had talked about expansion.

Lottie and Annie had often sat down with Kate and discussed the situation. The Tea Room and Lottieannie's were in the same category, size-wise. Each time they pledged to stick with their convictions: keep it small and remain human. What each woman had wanted was not wealth and fame, but recognition and a chance to work in an area she enjoyed. So, the days rolled by and the three of them remained sane.

• • •

Lad was happiest when Annie was working around home. He was chief assistant in the yard.

John got a new truck and was sharing its capabilities with the neighborhood. It was an '89 Chevy, with four-wheel drive, topper, slider window, and dual gas tanks. This reminded Annie that she must approach him about a possible trip to the U.P., to bring the canoe home. She didn't want to put it off until spring.

• • •

Through the grapevine Annie heard about a high school girl up the road about ten miles who gave horseback riding lessons. She had mentioned it to Frank, and he had shown an interest.

One of the days she was in the yard he came out of his place slamming the door. He called over, "Annie, you want to go check on that horse business? I've got to step away from this evil-eye computer."

Annie put Lad in the cottage, and she and Frank took off. She had jotted directions on a piece of scratch paper. Finally, they came across it. The land led back to a nice house with a couple of good-sized barns. It looked like a nice piece of land.

On her way to the door Annie had a feeling something was missing. The place had an empty atmosphere. She knocked on the door. A young girl answered. Annie made her inquiry. Ellie turned an ashen color. Annie was going to reach out to her when her eyes turned hateful. "My folks are in the barn. Talk to them." She slammed the door so that it vibrated. Annie heard her cry out as though she was in agony.

Her first reaction was to run to the truck and ask Frank to drive out of there. Instead, she motioned for him to shut off the motor. He got out of the truck and fell in step beside her. Annie filled him in and they headed for the barn.

They stepped in through the door. In the shadows they saw the couple embracing. They pulled apart and stared at Annie and Frank. Annie apologized. "It was unforgivable, we didn't even knock, or call out." The woman returned her arm to her husband's waist.

He said, "I'm sorry, I can't put on a false front anymore. This downsizing garbage is killing me. I had a good job. They let half of the staff go. We're all floundering. I've worked every day at anything I can pick up. I don't care what I do as long as I can take care of my family. I love these horses as much as our daughter does, but I can't feed them and us, too. They will have to be sold."

"I stopped at the house, that's why we knew where to find you. I'm worried about your daughter."

The woman stepped forward. "I have tried to be strong for each of them, but I'm running low on courage. Our girl doesn't understand. She seems to think we are deliberately removing her one bit of happiness. She won't listen to explanations. The situation is tearing our family apart. I don't know what to do."

Annie asked, "Could I see these horses?"

The mother rushed to the house. The man took Annie and Frank through the second barn where the stalls were. In a pasture behind the barn, six healthy, well-groomed horses were grazing. They came up to the door out of curiosity. One nuzzled up against Annie.

"How much are you asking for them?"

"I haven't been able to make my mind go that far yet."

"Well, you, your wife and daughter get your heads together. I'll give you fifteen minutes to come up with a fair price. You must know their worth. I'll bring a cashier's check tomorrow morning. I'm afraid I don't have a place to keep them. But if I could rent pasture and stalls from you—they seem to get loving care here. That's very important with horses. Since they will be mine, I'll pay for feed and vet service, etc. I would also be interested in hiring your daughter to give me riding lessons. That was my reason for coming here in the first place. Now I'm going to the house to fetch Ellie and Edna."

When Annie walked away even Frank was left stunned. Finally, he came to his senses. "What kind of work do you do?" He quickly located the paper he'd wadded up in his pocket. "Mr. Greensmith?"

David Greensmith was shaking himself like he was trying to wake up from a dream. The question finally arrived at its destination. He shrugged his shoulders and said, "I can do amazing things with computers. It's a talent everyone seems to have these days. Few jobs, but lots of capable people to fill them." Conversing was beginning to pull him out of the doldrums.

"I don't do home calls when interviewing. Could you be at my place of business at ten o'clock tomorrow? By that time Annie could have your check also. No guarantee, but I'd like to see what you can do."

"She's your wife then?"

Frank hesitated, then replied, "Next door neighbor."

The man looked at him and said, "Is this real?" He reached over and touched Frank on the arm. "You feel like a live person."

The three females arrived in the yard at the same time the men did.

Annie said, "We are going to the truck. In a few minutes I need that figure on the horses." Frank told her the arrangement he had made with Mr. Greensmith.

The three of them moved closer to the truck. David Greensmith estimated a figure.

"Sold. By the way, I won't be able to keep these horses forever. When you get on your feet you can buy them back. I'll sell at the same price I'm paying. See you soon, Edna. Ellie, we'll work up a schedule for the lessons."

The truck took off down the lane, leaving three people in shock.

When they reached the main road Annie moved closer to Frank, saying, "Well, aren't we a pair?" He slowed the truck and put his arm around her shoulder.

"Why did you do that? That's a lot of money."

"I've been wanting a horse. That's what money is for, to help people out of a jam. The papers say times are good. They are asking the wrong people. If you looked around you could see how well they keep the place.

It was their spirit that had hit the skids. Can't have neighbors goin' down the tube in despair. You get down at the bottom and it's too slippery to climb out." That night Annie wrote in her journal:

> Purchased 3 beautiful horses (temporary ownership only). Price undisclosed.

The bank door opened at 9:00 and Annie was first one at the window. She took the check for Mr. Greensmith over to Frank. "Will you pass this on to David? I need to go down and see John about something. David might feel better about accepting it from you."

When she reached John's she got right to the point: the ride to the Upper Peninsula. "I'd be delighted to drive you to the U.P. Lad can fit in the back."

Annie jumped up and down like a kid. "I hadn't even thought about Laddie." John insisted she call Joe Silvers from his place so plans could be made immediately. They decided to leave in the morning.

Annie sat at her desk reading her journal. Lad's chin was resting on her foot. She would have a devil of a time getting the chair moved back so she could get up. If she sat in a chair he was usually lying in between the four legs. Little rascal.

She couldn't even comprehend what she was reading about the past month. It was like going to a movie and watching the story of someone's life in two hours. She fell sound asleep with her head on the desk. She woke at midnight and went into the bathroom. Looking in the mirror, she saw the imprint of the journal binding etched in her cheek.

 CHAPTER 13

Lad and Annie were at John's early. Little sleep, an aching back, and a missed breakfast made her cranky. They weren't down the road a mile when the young woman and her dog were sound asleep, Annie leaning against the window and Lad curled in some blankets in the back.

John cleared his throat loud enough to wake her, suggesting coffee and a doughnut. She thought it sounded like a great idea.

After giving Lad a break from the topper on the truck bed, they were back on the road. "Where are you going to store the canoe, Annie?"

"Uh-oh: my competency points just plummeted."

"I've got a storage building out by the pens. It's pretty dusty in there, but you could throw some old sheets over it until spring."

"John, what would I do without you to rescue me?"

When they arrived at the turnoff of the dirt road, Snow was at the mailbox. Annie scrambled out of the truck. She introduced herself and Snow reached for both of her hands.

John drove on after a smile and wave.

The two women remained silent until the dust from the truck tires settled.

Joe had been right; Snow was a beautiful young woman. Annie hesitated to speak, wondering if Snow was an extremely shy person. Then she noticed there were tears in her eyes.

At last, she spoke. "We have looked forward to your visit, and yet I have dreaded it. For when the canoe goes it will be the closing of a memory that is so dear to us."

"No, I did not come to take away such a precious treasure. Those memories will remain with you forever. I didn't know Michael like you and Joe did. But the thoughts I carry in my heart cannot be removed.

"I was so thrilled with Joe's visit, and now I have the opportunity to meet you and little Joey." With that they began to move, at a faster pace, toward where John's truck was parked. The dust that blew up from the road settled on their shoulders as common understanding.

By the time Joe and John spotted the Annie and Snow, it was obvious that there was a growing friendship in progress. They appeared to have been old friends who were catching up after a lengthy separation.

In the yard Joe did the formal introductions. "Who is that peeking around from behind you?" asked Annie.

"Come on, Hiller, you will like these folks." The dog came around and leaned up against his master's leg.

"I've brought him a playmate." Annie picked up the sleepy Lad and put him on the ground. That ended the shyness. The two dogs went romping off.

Then Snow came back out with Joey, who was still waking up from his nap. They walked to a small building and Joe opened the doors wide to let the sun in.

Annie could not believe her eyes. She had never seen a canoe of such beauty and craftsmanship. She could hear Joe's voice in the background explaining details to John. She kept circling it and reaching out with her hands to touch its smoothness. As she examined the cane seats, Snow and

Joey came and stood next to her. "The caning is my offering to the finished project."

"Snow, I didn't dream it would look like this."

"There has not been one like this before, nor will there be another. The design was sent up in smoke at a ceremony just between my Josephs and me. It is a tribute to a special friend."

"I will hesitate to put it in the water in the spring."

"You must never do that. It must be a useful symbol. It will move through the water like magic."

Snow's melodious voice told its story as Annie closed her eyes and ran her hands once more along its sides. "It is twelve feet long. If you travel by yourself, turn the canoe around and paddle from the bow seat. Joey and I were with Joe when it was tested. It tracks well even in a strong crosswind. It is stable and safe to stand in. Hiller went with us that day also. It seemed only fitting."

Snow guided Annie's hand along the gunwales. "This is made of mahogany. Your paddles are one-piece ash beaver tail."

Annie opened her eyes again. "It's the design of the different woods that make it so striking. It seems wrong to accept such a gift."

"No, it is right that it should be yours."

With pride Joe showed them his different workshop areas and what was in progress.

Retiring to the house for supper, Annie and Lad played with little Joey. Later, Joe and Snow opened the sofa for John, and Annie slept in Joey's room on a cot.

In the morning the canoe was lifted, carefully laid on some soft discarded packing material, and secured.

As the said their good-byes, Annie remarked, "I am surprised Michael did not speak of you all."

Joe took her hand. "Not enough time. Not enough time for any of us."

Annie kissed Joey on his cheek and held Snow's hand tightly. "We will keep in touch." She patted Hiller on the head and scooped up Lad. As she climbed in the cab of the truck she called out, "I hope it doesn't rain or snow on my canoe." Even Joe laughed at that remark.

That evening Annie described the canoe and its builders in her journal. 'This canoe should be displayed in a museum. Its beauty is a gift for all eyes to behold. The man who designed it created a masterpiece.'

A couple of days later Annie was pulling out of her drive and Frank into his; they rolled their windows down. Frank called out, "Why didn't you let me know you needed a ride north?"

"Never thought of asking you."

"John tells me you picked up a canoe. Maybe we could glide up Pigeon Creek some summer day."

Annie hesitated, then finally said, "Maybe."

They each went on their way, each involved in personal thoughts.

 CHAPTER 14

In Annie's talks to Lottie, she found out that Lottie and her intended needed a bigger nest egg before the marriage would take place. Lottie would stay put, and business would go on as usual. Maybe in a few years there would be some changes. But for the present it was satisfactory all around. It was a relief to not have to tackle a change in the business right now. It was November, and holiday orders were piling up.

A salesman stopped in to the Confectionery, and he and Annie went down the street to that quiet corner in the Tea Room to sit and talk about future supplies. There was an out of the way table that Kate tried to keep free for them. A wonderful place for their breaks. It was also a pleasant spot for short business meetings. Having the Tea Room just three shops away made it almost too convenient for Lottie and Annie. Annie often repaid Kate's consideration by filling in for her if Kate needed to be away. Their friendship overlapped into the business world.

When Annie returned, Lottie kept looking at her and smiling. "What's with you, Lottie?"

"Your neighbor called and I told him you were out on a luncheon date with a gentleman friend. I asked if he wanted you to return his call. He said 'No!' and hung up."

"Frank has never called here. Do you suppose something is wrong?"

"No, and don't you call him. If there had been an emergency he would have told me."

"Why did you tell him I had a luncheon date?"

"Annie, are you a first-class jerk?"

Later, when Annie unlocked the back door of her cottage, the phone started ringing. "Hello."

"It's Frank. I was wondering if you would be interested in going out to supper?"

"Well, I just walked in the house."

"I know that. We'll go someplace nice."

"Have you found a young lady you want to impress, and you are going to wine and dine me as a practice run?"

"That must be it."

Annie thought he sounded put out with her. "If you will give me an hour, I'll shower and put a pretty dress on, and wear perfume and everything. That way you'll get the right atmosphere."

"One hour."

When she got a good look at Frank in the lighted parking lot Annie said, "My, don't you look nice," slipping her arm through his. "I hope this girl is deserving of this extra effort on your part."

He looked at her in a funny way and said, "She is." Then he reached around and laid his other hand on top of hers.

It was turning into a lovely evening. Between the entree and dessert Annie excused herself and went to the restroom. She took her purse and freshened up her hair and lipstick.

Frank couldn't take his eyes from her as she wound her way back to the table. She stopped several times to speak to friends. He had not seen her dressed in evening wear before. She was stunning and graceful, and . . .

"Hello, Frank, how's the business going?"

Frank stood and shook hands with the businessman, and there was an exchange of conversation.

The spell was broken. After dessert and coffee they drove home in a relaxed state, listening to soft music on the truck radio. Annie invited him in for coffee, but he asked for a rain check. He would take what luck he'd had and not push it.

As each readied for bed they thought back over the evening. It had been so pleasant, but then had ended rather abruptly. Neither of them was happy with the ending. Neither was ready for it to end. Their lights went out. Their lights went on. Each read until the wee hours of the morning. Lights were turned off again and there was restless tossing and turning. And the moon, peeping through their windows, smiled. For the man in the moon had observed this scene many times before.

 CHAPTER 15

On Saturday, as agreed, Annie drove to the Greensmiths' to meet Ellie Greensmith in the barn. They were to set up plans for Annie's private riding instructions.

Upon arriving, Annie was barely out of the car when Edna came running from the house to detain her. She clasped Annie's hand with both of her own.

"God bless you, Annie Tucker. You have been in our prayers all week. What a fine Christian friend God has sent us." Annie was uncomfortable with this but made no comment. She smiled and quickly moved to the barn area.

Annie told Ellie of her short but pleasant experience with horses in North Carolina.

"This is what I had in mind," said Annie, explaining her wishes. She wanted to learn to ride, but first she wanted to learn about the horse itself. Her desires were not to be afraid, to be able to handle with confidence a creature so large. There had to be trust and understanding between the horse and rider and the instructor.

When Ellie started to explain her passion for horses, everything else was forgotten. "One thing," she said. "I want to apologize for the way I acted when you came by that day. I had wanted a horse for so long and finally we had horses. It was like a dream. Then a short time later the dream was gone. I didn't get the whole picture. I was thinking of one person, me. Like it was all my folks' fault. I didn't know how to handle it."

Annie placed her hand on Ellie's arm. "I've had a little trouble with things like that myself lately. What do you say if we both start from a new beginning." They agreed upon the price and lesson times. Annie left the lesson with a feeling of contentment. It would be a learning relationship, all around.

• • •

On the way home from work on Monday, Annie saw Frank's truck backed up to Maude's door. After she had been home a few minutes she became concerned that something might be wrong. She dialed Maude's number. Maude assured her that everything was fine, and please come over right away as something very exciting was taking place. No one could resist an invitation like that. Annie walked in and Maude wheeled out to the kitchen to greet her. She grabbed her hand, pulling her toward the front room.

In the corner of the living room Frank was so deep in concentration he didn't even notice her presence. Annie's mouth gaped open. "My gosh, Maude, I have never seen anything quite like this before. This is state-of-the-art equipment. It's more complicated than anything I've ever used."

"I called Frank a while back saying I wanted to learn about the use of a simple computer. We've been talking about this for a month or so. He took me down to his place and showed me some basic stuff."

Frank turned around. "This woman is a whiz. We both got so excited about the project we forgot to tell anyone."

"Frank showed me how I could communicate with people all over the globe." Then she sat up straight and proud. "Before the week is out I shall be employed. May even go on a shopping spree and buy myself a couple of snappy outfits. I know these people won't see me but I need to look the part."

"Maude is going to be my first secretary. I told her I might even take her to one of the conventions to show her off. It's an incentive program I've devised."

Annie shook her head in disbelief. "Congratulations, Maude. What a fine surprise. Aren't we all lucky that Mr. Frank King moved into our neighborhood?" She walked over and gave him a big kiss and hug. Backing away from him she sheepishly said, "Sorry."

Frank turned back to what he had been doing. Maude and Annie moved to the kitchen. "Frank says it will be a train-as-you-work program. He promises not to overload me with work. How nice it will be to feel tired when I go to bed at night. It will be satisfying to feel like I deserve a rest at the end of the day." Her eyes sparkled as she spoke.

Frank called out, "Almost finished for the day, Annie. I'll give you a lift home."

Chapter 16

As he pulled up by his door Annie said, "I'll expect you for supper in half an hour. Nothing fancy." The day before she had prepared homemade stew. Biscuits and a fresh green salad with ranch dressing, plus ice cream and cookies, would do the trick. They spent the time talking about Maude's new project. "What a wonderful thing for you to do, Frank."

"I can't take credit for any of it. It just began to take shape. You know Maude when she even gets an inkling of an idea."

As Frank was leaving he paused at the door for a second but then moved on outside. "A great meal, Annie. Thanks."

Rosa called on Wednesday. "Annie, would you like to go to church with me on Sunday?"

"Are you still going downtown?"

There was a slight pause. "I've been doing something different lately."

"Could you explain that?"

"It will be obvious. You would have to pick me up at a quarter of seven. Oh, yes, you'll need five dollars."

"Is this some kind of a special service? It sounds rather mysterious. I'm uncomfortable with far-out stuff, you know. But I'll pick you up. I can't think you would be into any strange goings-on."

"You don't have to dress up, and don't eat any breakfast."

Nothing was mentioned the balance of the week, and Annie was completely baffled.

On Sunday Annie drove into Rosa's driveway. Rosa hurried out of the house with a big smile on her face.

"I never thought to ask you where this place was located," Annie said.

"Drive up to the Landing."

"Now you've really got me. There's no church there. What's going on?"

When they arrived they saw light shining from the window of the little private dining room. They could see lights on in the kitchen, too.

Just before Annie opened the door to go inside, Rosa said, "Just be yourself, follow along, and observe." Having no time to dispute, Annie stepped inside with a blank look on her face.

"Hey, Rosa, see you made it today. Nice to see you again, Annie. Do you remember me? We were fishing buddies, way back. You always were a piperoo. I live in the little brown house on Pigeon Creek." As recognition registered on her face, and she smiled, Edward gave her a hearty handshake.

Annie noticed that the others were dropping their money in a bowl on the counter, so she followed suit. The aroma coming from the back was fabulous.

A couple of tables were set up in fine fashion. Pierre pushed through the door to show off the most beautifully prepared omelet Annie had ever seen. Parsley and twisted orange slices were around the platter. Rosa poured coffee and Annie fell into line as the rest of them went into the kitchen and carried out fresh fruit and toast. She grabbed the butter and jam.

They sat down, ate heartily, complimenting the chef. Everyone pitched in to help straighten up and put the dishes in the back. They talked about the activities that were going on in the area.

Afterward, coats and hats were put back on, on and everyone walked out the door. Even Pierre put on his coat and boots and got bundled up. Some went to their cars and left for home. Two of the men walked down a path in the woods. Annie, Rosa, and Pierre went down to the dock where the fishing boats were tied up in the summer. They commented on the ice fishermen with their bright orange outfits. Pierre said he needed to get back.

Annie and Rosa returned to the car and drove home in silence. As Rosa got out, she asked if Annie would like to come in for tea. The motor was shut off and Annie walked quietly into the house behind her. Still nothing was said, but there was no awkward feeling to the silence, just a peaceful feeling. Rosa hung her coat in the closet and Annie laid hers on the back of a chair. After the tea was brewed, Rosa joined Annie at the kitchen table.

"Rosa, did I miss something?"

Rosa looked up and smiled. "I don't think you did."

"I am totally confused."

"Did you miss the singing, the organ, announcements, the bulletin, or the stained glass windows? Or was it the fact that no one asked you to join a group, or be on a committee, or the joining of hands as you stood in a circle to pray?"

The look in Annie's eyes changed.

Rosa said, "Tell me, what did you notice?"

"The gathering of friends, good food, cooperation, no one was in charge, appreciation of the outdoors."

Rosa continued, "Also it was mentioned that there was a single mother to the north of us who is having a rough time. I'll have to make some cookies and take them to her next week. I imagine the men went into the woods to see if there were any trees down that they could cut up. They could stack some for her to use next year. I wouldn't be surprised if they took some from their own wood piles to get her through for her immediate needs. I'm sure they will at least see that her wood box is full for her fireplace. We heard she was using that for her main heat. Most likely someone will drop by her place with a couple of bags of groceries."

Tears came to Annie's eyes. "It was all there, wasn't it, Rosa, in its purest sense? Nothing false or demanding. Just there in the open, for us to step forward and respond."

"It came about a few months back. Several of us had stopped at the Landing for coffee after church. Each of us was grumbling about one small thing or another.

"It was Pierre's idea. He expressed his opinion that prayer was a private thing. It started a big discussion. He suggested that we come there on Sunday morning, and jokingly called it Church at the Landing.

"There is no real name, no rules. We try to give him an idea of how many to plan on. If an outsider sees the lights and stops in for breakfast, that's just dandy. The restaurant opens later on Sunday, so it's no problem. Most of us still attend our traditional churches also. The average attendance at the Landing is half a dozen or so.

"A while back there was an old gent, lives toward town. Someone got wind of the fact that he was worried because his back door needed fixing. That Monday a couple of the guys just happened by with the right equipment in the back of their truck and took care of things."

Annie thanked Rosa. She put her tea cup in the kitchen and said her good-byes. She backed out and drove the car down her own driveway. She went inside and sat looking out the window, forgetting to remove her coat. After a while, she took off her coat and put it away. Sitting down again in the same chair, she shook her head in wonderment. Then she closed her eyes for a minute and uttered, "You are full of surprises, aren't you, God?" She had gone regularly to the Methodist church in Tuckerville when she was a child. As an adult she often attended only about once a month. She still enjoyed visiting with all the old friends.

• • •

Annie was falling behind in her journal again. The riding lessons were going well. David Greensmith was putting in a lot of hours for Frank's computer business, and it was growing. Things seemed to be going much better for that family. And Maude not only had a view of the road and the lake, but a view of the world.

The second week in December the mail contained an invitation to attend a get-together at Rosa's on December 15th.

When Annie arrived at Rosa's, the party was well underway, full of conversation and news about plans for the winter months and holidays. Rosa's family and some friends from town were there, and everyone was enjoying the good food. Annie looked up and saw John and Rosa standing side by side holding hands. She became silent and cocked her head to one side. Gradually, everyone ceased talking. Rosa took John's other hand and announced, "John and I were married this morning in the church office."

The first one to jump up was Annie, and she wrapped her arms about them both. "I don't know when I've ever heard such happy news. I think we should clear out and leave the happy couple alone."

Rosa's granddaughter piped up and said, "They will be lonesome if they are alone."

"Oh, no, they won't. Two people who love each other are not lonesome when they are together." Annie started putting her warm things on. "I need to go for a walk."

Frank removed his jacket and hat from the hook in the hallway, and took off after her. "It's dark out. You can't walk alone."

They walked on a familiar trail in the woods. Annie could not contain her joy for the happy couple. "Two people couldn't deserve to be together more."

"You seem to approve of marriage. Why aren't you hitched to somebody?"

"No one has asked me."

"Maybe someone has, but you didn't recognize the offer."

Annie felt sick to her stomach. "Well, Mr. Big Businessman, I am quite capable of recognizing a proposal, in business or personal."

And she was gone. Frank turned every which way but did not see her fleeing through the trees. A forest nymph for sure. It was as if she had been drawn up in the trees and hidden by Robin Hood and his merry men. "Dang it! You blew it again, Frank old man. Are you ever going to learn how to treat this woman properly?" With that, he turned and walked home alone, feeling very lonesome.

 CHAPTER 17

December was a month of pure madness at the store. It was difficult for Annie to have energy left at the close of the day for writing in her journal. Annie looked forward to spring so she could enjoy riding the horses outside. She would have liked to take Lad with her to the barns, but for various reasons never suggested it. Also, in the spring there would be the unveiling of the canoe. Maybe she could plan a launching party. She might even take old Frank E. for his ride.

Christmas cards were arriving. Most exciting was one from Ma. Ma claimed the girls were getting sick of looking at her. They said when spring hit she was to get out, to go see Annie. P.S. Poncho was losing some of his fire. Annie dropped the card on the floor and danced all through the house. What a wonderful promise of a new year. In the spring Ma would come to visit. No one had to know why they were such good friends. They would have a picnic and invite her family from Maude's View, Lottie and her fella, and Kate, too. "Thank you, Santa Claus, a fine gift, indeed."

Maude called at work one day. "I need to go to the bank. My cleaning girl could drop me off. Could you pick me up at noon? You would have to come inside and get me. Then we could have some lunch."

"A break would be good for me."

Annie stepped in the door of the bank and thought, I can't deal with this wild woman. She practically fell into the big comfortable chair across from Maude. "What is the plan here? Aren't you going to get us into real trouble this time?"

"It was their idea. My girl and I were in when they opened this morning. The teller who let me into my safety deposit box and I were discussing the frigid weather. I looked at the fireplace, the inviting fire and chairs. By golly, I'm going home and get the book I'm reading and come back and spend the day in this snug spot. Those were my exact words.

"When I got to the door she called out, 'Why not, and bring your lunch.' So, my girl and I stopped at the grocery and bought some supplies. We scurried around, and here I am."

"Maude, what are these people going to think?"

"I made cupcakes for everyone. They're happy as magpies. Here, have a bologna sandwich. I get a big package of sliced bologna—that suits me best—and grind it up with pimento, then add some mayonnaise." She dug around in her basket. "Here we go, festive Christmas plates and napkins."

They picnicked in the homey lobby of their neighborhood bank. They laughed so hard all the way home that their stomachs hurt. "Maude, how do you think up these capers?"

"It wasn't me; it was that clever little cutie at the bank."

"I hope we didn't get her fired."

"Oh, send some chocolates to the bank president. Put a thank you note on it." And the laughter started up anew.

Annie tried to write the incident in her journal but couldn't stop laughing. Then she became sober and wrote: Maude's Christmas gift. What a special family. She loved them all.

December 17th Annie drove to the church at Holly's Landing. Frank was already there. The small dining room was festive. Pierre had recently added candles to the tables. After they had eaten, Pierre started playing Christmas music on his phonograph. He was having a great time announcing the titles he had chosen. They started with traditional carols, and everyone joined in singing. Following that were a few silly jingles. Then a couple of pretty tunes.

Annie was showing the older men how to dance with Maude in her wheelchair and make it pleasant for both participants.

Then Pierre turned the lights down low. The candles changed the look of the room, and the atmosphere. "This is a record I found at a garage sale last summer. It's one of those records from GOODYEAR, 1974; this is side 2. It says, 'Candlelight, a change of mood.' Very pretty."

When the slow music started, one of the men danced with Maude. Then Rosa and John took a turn at the next number. Another slow one, about the promises of Christmas, followed.

Frank asked Annie to dance. It was the kind of song that makes you smile and look at your neighbors, nodding in agreement with the words. The next piece offered a slow jazz beat. Frank and Annie danced the way they had that first day in the yard. They forgot the others were there. But the others were there, watching and wondering.

They danced close. The ending was lovely. Frank and Annie stood for a moment after the phonograph stopped playing. Annie's head was against his chest as he held her gently. Frank did not want to step away from her. But he took her arm and guided her back to where she had been sitting and said, "Thank you," seating her very carefully.

"Merry Christmas everyone," was shouted all around.

The first person out the door stuck his head back inside. "The swans are in."

Annie hurried with her coat. Rosa and Frank were talking, so Annie ran ahead and caught up with John.

As Annie and John walked toward the water, Frank and Rosa could hear the two of them talking. Their voices drifted clearly through the cold air.

"Swans return to nest in the same territory. They prefer shallow water.

That makes it easier for them to feed on the water plants because they can lower their long necks under the water and reach them. They also mate for life."

Rosa took Frank's arm. "When are you going to tell her?"

"Tell her?"

"How much you love her."

"Is it that obvious?"

"To everyone but you and Annie."

"Doesn't she know?"

"You have to tell a woman. Everyone Annie has truly held dear has been taken from her. She's afraid to love, unless she knows for sure. Do I think she loves you? I think she loves you more than she is willing to admit to herself. It's up to you now."

Frank stopped. "I was planning to visit my family in Chicago over the holidays. I wasn't thinking of leaving until midweek. I've changed my mind. I'm going home and pack and leave within the hour. There're some business meetings and contacts I need to deal with seriously. Good-bye and thank you." He kissed Rosa on the cheek.

When John and Annie heard Frank's car door they turned and waited for Rosa to come up even with them. The three of them joined arms.

Rosa said, "Frank is heading for Chicago until after the holidays."

"He seems preoccupied," Annie said. "I didn't know he was going today. I didn't even wish him a Happy Holiday . . . a Merry Christmas . . . a safe trip home. . . . Nothing."

"You are coming for Christmas dinner, aren't you, Annie?"

• • •

The next week was a killer at work. Annie missed Frank. She didn't like to look in the direction of his house and see no lights in the window. Phooey, it wasn't the lights; she just missed Frank.

On December 24th Annie attended her own church. There were lots of friendly Hello's and Season's Greetings. Annie wrapped her gifts for Rosa and John after returning home.

She had not had time to call after they had settled in at John's. When she arrived on Christmas day she was surprised. With the addition of Christmas decorations, on top of the other changes, she couldn't believe her eyes. "Rosa, should you change a man's castle this much?"

"He said I was to change his castle into a home. So, I added color everywhere, and we love it."

Annie left early. She had to take Lad for a little walk. The 26th would be dreadful at work. The Christmas spirit would have passed by. The day-after purchases would take care of gifts forgotten. The Confectionery had to have ample supply to cover the demand. And, yes, each must have just the right packaging. Sometimes people felt obligated to give these gifts. But there were also those who were there to pick out something for that special someone. That made the day worthwhile.

• • •

As Annie headed home from the store on the day after Christmas, she could feel the storm coming. It was going to be nasty. But it was Annie and Lottie's practice to be closed on the 27th to get a real day of rest, and Annie was grateful for that.

When she got home Annie took care of Lad. She built up a long-lasting fire and had stacked lots of wood inside. She wanted the warmth right through tomorrow. She had a couple of good books and plenty of food. Let it storm.

She had just curled up to read when she heard the back door rattle. At first she sat motionless. Lad opened his eyes but remained relaxed, so Annie got up to check out the noise.

She opened the door to her very own Abominable Snowman. She pulled him inside and latched the door. "Frank, I didn't think you were returning until after the first of the year. What are you doing out in such a storm?"

"My mother kicked me out. Said I was a mess, and to go home where I belonged. Didn't you miss me?"

"Miss you? Of course I did. But how did you gather this much snow between your car and my back door?"

"I've been walking in the woods."

"That is a bad idea on a night like this."

"I was rehearsing."

"No wonder your mother sent you back. You've gone mad. Let me put the tea kettle on so we can get something warm in your stomach. Then we'll remove some of those clothes."

Annie turned toward the stove and froze. Outside the window, the wind was whipping the snow around in strange patterns. She saw them. Snow ghosts. A woman, a younger man, and a dog. They were the likenesses of Aunt Mary, Michael, and Lass. They appeared together as though in a family portrait. Then they were gone. They were there only an instant. She had seen them. They were together. It was like a release, a message: love again, love again.

The tea kettle began to sing and so did Annie's heart. She turned the burner off and swung back toward Frank. He had removed some of his outer clothing.

Annie knelt at his feet and tapped one of his knees. "Raise your foot and let me help you off with your boots, my friend."

Frank placed his cold hands on each side of her cheeks. "I did not come here for your friendship. I want you to be my wife. I love you. I want us to be married."

Annie began to laugh.

"Did I say it wrong?"

"I just want it on the record that I did recognize your offer."

"I don't have a ring for you."

"Not to worry. I'll remember."

Frank pulled Annie to his lap. The water dripping off his clothes had made the floor slippery and the chair tumbled over. Finally, they wrestled the wet boots off, and the laughter subsided.

They had moved into the other room by the cozy fire. Pulling Annie into the circle of his arms, Frank smiled as he looked into her eyes. "Woman, I'm going to kiss you and I am not going to stop for a long long time."

Annie nestled within his arms. Inside the walls of the cottage was tenderness, caring, and love. Outside, the winds of the world whistled. But for two people, love blocked out all fury and sound.

About the Author

As a young girl Donna Bocks wrote poetry emulating her beloved Auntie. While in college her oral storytelling was popular with roommates—"tell us a story" was the constant request. When her children arrived, Donna loved to rock them in the rocking chair and sing original story-songs spun from their everyday lives. Her literary impulses were piqued by an author interview. Afterward she realized that she could actually write down the stories in her head.

Most of Donna's novels are set in Michigan where she was born 78 years ago. "Stories happen," says Donna, "walking everyday in the neighborhood. The houses begin to speak and the stories grow street by street, house by house." Donna's oldest son asked her to take him on a walk and point out the elements of one of her novels. He was delighted as street names became names of characters, and as his familiar surroundings were sprinkled with his mother's magic storytelling dust!

The author welcomes correspondence from her readers:
P. O. Box 8231, Holland, Michigan 49422-8231.
DonnaBocks@birthAbook.com

About the Illustrator

Tom Ball has always loved to draw. He studied art and architectural drawing throughout high school. To relieve the intensity of his chosen profession in law enforcement, he draws. When the family goes camping, he sketches, and his daughter does too. Tom is a two-time Olympian, having served on security details at both the Atlanta and Salt Lake City Olympics. He is the husband of Colleen, father of Travis and Sarah, and proud walker of Aspen, an English Springer Spaniel.